Making the Impossible Difficult

Making the Impossible Difficult

Tools for Getting Unstuck

Edited by
John H. Frykman
Thorana S. Nelson

iUniverse, Inc.
New York Lincoln Shanghai

Making the Impossible Difficult
Tools for Getting Unstuck

iUniverse, Inc.

For information address:
iUniverse, Inc.
2021 Pine Lake Road, Suite 100
Lincoln, NE 68512
www.iuniverse.com

Illustrations by Lee Becker

ISBN: 0-595-29712-9

Printed in the United States of America

dedicated to our

spouses:
Cheryl Arnold
Victor Nelson

children:
Kristin
Lars
Erik
Travis
Stacy

grandchildren:
Charlotte
Kyle
Taylor
Deryk

with love and thankfulness for making the impossible miraculous

Contents

Preface

Thorana Nelson

When he first invited me to work with him on this book, John said it was about getting unstuck from life's calamities. The current title, *Making the Impossible Difficult: Tools for Getting Unstuck* says it better. Before we can get unstuck, we often must come to some sort of realization that the situation is hopeless. It's only impossible (to paraphrase Watzlawick), when we stay stuck.

John and I both have experienced calamities of all sorts; all of us have. Not many people stay stuck in them, however, and the more we help each other discover or rediscover ways of getting out of the impossible box of hopelessness and no possibilities of change, the more we help each other in our humanity. Sharing brings connection, connection breeds ideas, and ideas and action get us unstuck: the viewing and doing of life. New viewings, new doings change stuckness into possibilities for acceptance and change.

And that's what this book is all about: stories, essays, and poems about life, about accepting and doing and viewing and reviewing so that what seems impossible becomes merely difficult.

When I think about the calamities in my life, I have either forgotten the hopeless and impossible ones or they were transformed into new meanings and doings. Sometimes I've learned to welcome them as friends to be embraced rather than enemies to be fought or avoided. Or maybe they weren't calamities after all; maybe they were just difficult situations and challenges. I can't find a pattern to how I have managed to survive them or transform them. I just did what I could at the time and trusted that somehow, someway, something would happen. It came to pass, not to stay.

The stories and essays and poems in this book help us see how our commonness, our ability to be with each other, often moves us from the impossible to the merely difficult. Some parts may seem that they are all about self, about the writer, the artist. But these authors have courageously chosen to share these pieces, to give them to all of us so that we can know them, their situations, their ways of getting unstuck. They are not meant to be analyzed; they are windows through which we can see with new eyes the stuck places, broken places, healing places. And, perhaps to spark an idea or two for our own calamities and difficult times.

We hope that you enjoy this book. It was John's idea and reflects much of John's life as a person—pastor, author, therapist, friend—and I can't think of anyone I'd rather have done this with. We couldn't find a publisher—we've had many other calamities along the way—so John said, let's self-publish and found a way to do that. He had health problems, I had work problems, but neither of us gave up. And when it came time to put it together, two years after recruiting our authors, they were still with us, excited, pleased, and encouraging by being prompt in providing us with what we needed. John, with his good humor, helped whenever I screamed or faltered.

And it's done. So, we want you to sit back with your favorite drink or pet or friend and thumb through this book. Don't try to figure out why we included something, what the author meant, or what it means for your life. Let your right brain take it in, integrate it with all your other life experience, and use it however it will.

Here's to getting UNSTUCK!

September 2003

Becker

Introduction

John H. Frykman

Life, Near Death, New Life

On a windy April afternoon, dressed in a costume to look like a prince, with a diagonal red satin sash across his chest, an eight-year-old boy strolled happily down a country road on his way to rendezvous with his parents. He could see his father's gray Chevrolet in the distance, his father seated behind the wheel smoking a cigar.

There were half-a-dozen German Shepherd dogs playing in the freshly cut cornfield to his right, chasing round and round in a circle. As he approached them, they suddenly turned on him and attacked him. They were biting him on the head, arms, legs, tearing the flesh, tossing him about as if he were a rag doll, simple prey.

But he felt no pain (not knowing he had gone into shock). They dragged him and tossed him and bit him for more than one hundred yards across that newly cut cornfield. Then, as if sent by God, an old woman appeared, coming out of the house at the end of the field. She had a long smoking iron poker in her hand.

Mrs. Salley strode fearlessly toward the pack of dogs and the young boy, whacking the dogs with the poker as she encountered them. Eventually, they ran whimpering away. She picked up the lifeless form of the little boy and carried him into her house and telephoned for an ambulance to come and take him to the hospital.

The boy could hear the nurses talking in the corridor outside his room. "He'll never walk again." "It's a wonder he is still alive." "It will be a miracle if he lives!"

The story of the attack was front-page news. There was a large picture of the boy with his mangled and mauled face.

The dogs were destroyed by the gunfire of the local constables. The owners were of German heritage and this was a time of war.

Representatives of the Boston Red Sox came to visit the boy in the hospital and brought him a baseball autographed by the whole team. Names such as

Bobby Doerr, Jimmy Fox, Ted Williams. Ted Williams invited him to come to a game when he was well enough, and to sit with him in the player's dugout.

His mother read stories and books to him. She read and read and read and read. When she stopped, he would shout at her, "Read!" And she would.

He did not return to school that year…but, by Fall, he was well enough, he was walking, it was beyond belief, and returned to school.

This boy's life had been changed. His wounds became signs of a miracle. The caring of his parents, doctor, nurses, family, friends, neighbors, and strangers would never be forgotten.

He would go on to play on three high school championship football teams. Enter the university on an athletic scholarship. Play tennis. Participate in track, running the 880-yard race. Play baseball. Be on the debating team. Write poetry. Live as one glad to be alive.

That's what this book is about. It is not going to be about slick theories, sophisticated conceptualizations. It is about GETTING UNSTUCK! It is written with the belief that the natural, normal condition of a human being is to be doing well, to be coping well, to be dealing with the variety of calamities that are just part of life.

The group that made up the Brief Therapy Center at the Mental Research Institute in Palo Alto (John Weakland, Paul Watzlawick, Art Bodin, Richard Fisch) would often say, "Life is one goddam thing after another and quality of life is measured not by how free of problems you are but by how well you deal with the problems that come your way."

Too much of what goes on as psychotherapy, counseling, and psychiatry is based on someone's opinion of what is good to do, not what has been scientifically proven to be effective. And generally, the result of that kind of "help" is almost always the same. A third get better, a third get worse, and a third stay the same. To us, that's not good enough. It's time to admit that when help doesn't help, it isn't help!

So many times, when someone is in trouble, they are like the proverbial "broken record." They keep repeating the same unsuccessful strategies for coping with a problem. And it doesn't work.

Most commonly, "If I only understood my problem, then I could deal with it." How many times has understanding helped you? Unless a person is willing to challenge what they are telling themselves about a problem, what they are doing about a problem, the problem continues as a game without end.

When I was smoking almost three packs of cigarettes a day, I knew and understood the part they played in my daily life. I couldn't get into a car and begin driving without lighting up! The understanding didn't help me one bit.

The day I stopped smoking was the day that I got "unstuck!" It wasn't easy, but it was the turning point, October 2, 1964. And I've not had another cigarette or cigar, or anything else to smoke, since! My "broken record" was interrupted by strep throat, a staph infection in the strep throat, and coming home from the hospital and feeling the powerful urge to go to the drawer where I kept my cigarettes to get one, even before talking to my wife or to my children. Suddenly and powerfully, I felt "unstuck!" It was not easy, it was hard, to say the least, but I never did smoke another cigarette, even to this very day. I truly believe that I would not be alive today if that serendipitous intervention had not happened.

Some years ago, Jack Annon and his colleagues at the University of Hawaii came up with the PLISSIT approach to sexual problems. To me it applies to all problems and is at the heart of all getting "unstuck" strategies. They said that for most problems, people only need Permission to be the way they are. For others, Limited Information will do the trick. For a few, Specific Suggestions are necessary. And, for less than five percent of the cases, Intensive Therapy is necessary. Permission, Limited Information (education), Specific Suggestions, Intensive Therapy, a great model for approaches that get people "unstuck" rather than trapped in "therapy with no end."

What is included in this book are contributions from friends, colleagues, clients, poets, and others—all examples of being able to get to get "unstuck!" They are windows open to a world of opportunity, a world where what is possible, even if possible with great difficulty, is the norm, rather than clinical, stuck, judgements about people and their problems.

August 2003

We Remember

In the pit,
Again.
I remember this place too well.
How I had hoped last time
    was the last time,
    but here I am
    again.

After so many years,
    you'd think I'd have a friend here,
But, no.
Only cold darkness,
eternal, unforgiving
darkness.
No light from above in this forsaken abyss,
    just the endless depth of
    darkness below.
Death would be kinder
    than this place.

And just before my soul
    relinquishes hope,
I remember.
I remember the sun's warmth on a winter's day.
I remember the sound of a friend's laughter.
I remember the eyes of compassion.
Then, suddenly there is a faint light,

It is an ancient friend
    I had long forgotten.
How could I have not remembered?
Who I am, where I come from,
    where I am to go.
I remember.

As the light grows,
I find a foothold here,
    a place to hold onto there.
Slowly, I make my way up,
    and out into the light.
Finally to rest.

As I make my way home
    to the faces I once knew
    to the new life before me,
The darkness of the pit fades into the mist—
    at last behind me.
But slowly too
    does the memory of the light fade
    into that same mist.
And the grayness settles in.
A constant hum,
    keeps me doing,
    not noticing light or dark;
    the mist offers an numbing comfort.

In a momentary pause,
    I touch another.
    I start to remember.
    life, light, and, yes, even the dark.

But, the moment passes,
    and, again,
    we quietly
    disappear into the mist.
My friend, come back,
    help me to remember.
I need you
    for me
    to remember.
Let us remember.

Diane Gehart

In the Midst of Calamity, Gratefulness and Love

Lisa Hanks-Baxter

It is ever amazing to me just how resilient people are. Life's calamities are many for everyone, but much more for some. As I've gotten older, I have realized how enriched our lives can potentially be, but that enrichment often grows out of the most painful of times. The other day I read an article in a magazine in which Christopher Reeves was saying that it was only after his accident and paralysis that he was able to open his eyes and his heart to a whole world of beautiful individuals. I have watched as Michael J. Fox has spoken about what his experience with Parkinson's has given to him. I have watched Americans who have gone to distant parts of the world to donate their time and services, only to step on land mines and have an arm and a leg blown off. They have come back from their personal tragedies only to tenaciously give more. I have seen my own husband courageously survive what could only be described as a brutal illness, come back from the brink of death, feeling lucky, grateful, and willing to give more. I have survived the worst times of my own life, feeling more grateful, more loving, more patient and more compassionate.

When we are in the midst of our own calamities, we tend to feel that no one can really understand how bad life can be. We feel overwhelmed by the reality of how much or how little we really can control. We don't want to hear about anybody else's experience. We don't want to hear people saying that things will be better, for even though they may be well-meaning, we feel that they really do not understand. Comments like, "there is light at the end of the tunnel" are met with irritation. There can be no hope of such a light, rather we are immersed in the belief that these devastating experiences can only leave bleeding, open, scar-ridden wounds. The intensity of these feelings can run deeper than we ever knew was possible. We are deeply engrossed in a process we never knew we had the capacity to live through. We dig down deep inside of our selves and find reservoirs we've never known we had. And most amazingly, at a certain depth, our

4

tragedies begin to transform themselves from something that has felt horrendous, to something that has given us the opportunity to live more fully. This process is not an easy one. And it has its own time schedule.

I was close to my mother. She was a wonderful, gentle, soft spoken but strong person. She died entirely too young. When she died, I thought I would too. I hadn't been close to my father for many years. Through the daze of my grief-ridden depression, I realized that she would never know any of my children, and more sadly, they would not get to know her. It was nearly more than I could bear. Interestingly enough, I didn't figure my father into this equation. Things had been so rocky and distant between us for so long that I couldn't foresee him being involved with his grandchildren. How wrong I was.

It was due to my mother's death that my father and I were able to deal with each other directly. We had no intermediary. Getting to know my father at this time in my life turned out to be a way of moving both of us through our grief. I think he went through this process in one way or another with each of his four children. As he and I got to know each other, we both were amazed to learn new things about my mother and about each of us in relationship to her. These revelations enriched our memories of her, and at the same time, brought my father and me closer than we had ever been. When my son was born, he had the most adoring grandfather a boy could ever hope for. My father died in all of his children's arms, loved as much as anyone could be by his children, his grandchildren, his nieces, nephews, and their families, and by his friends.

My husband John's illness has been the most difficult calamity I have faced. But I am learning that there really is light at the far end of some of those tunnels. Throughout my life I have been described as "sensitive" or "super sensitive." I now understand such sensitivity to be what I would now call "intuition." While being labeled sensitive has carried a somewhat negative connotation, I have since learned that it can be a very powerful source of strength. Although I carry my intuition mostly within myself psychologically, I have learned that it also can be carried physically.

As John wondered why his body had created such a cancer, something important shifted in me. For several months I had been feeling depressed and depleted. I had felt that something was dreadfully wrong, and I even had considered taking antidepressants. I had told John two weeks before that I was afraid that his foot and leg weren't healing because he might have cancer. I didn't know where that thought was coming from, but when we found out he did have cancer, my confusion and depression stopped. My "super sensitive nature" or intuition had kicked in and would not leave me alone. I knew that John could possibly be sick enough to die, but I strongly felt that we were two weeks ahead of the game. Other intuitive women in our family and friends had the same sense as I did. John came to depend on these feelings and dreams of ours; he found solace in them. When traditional allopathic medicine gave him only "six good months," we all felt strongly that that would probably not be the case. First we fired the pessimistic, gray-skinned and pale oncologist that felt he had the right to give us that "sentence." His narrow-mindedness would only keep him from helping his many patients for whom he could offer nothing. We soon found that there were alternatives, tried and true, in other countries as well as this one to be considered. The door that subsequently opened presented us with hope, faith, and gratefulness. Today, five years later, we have a wonderful network of friends, practitioners and doctors, allopathic and alternative, who have been successfully treating cancer patients for a long time. The view we have of cancer has changed drastically from a death sentence to a chronic condition that can be dealt with as aggressively as we are able. As I write this, John's scans are clear of any tumors.

John's sickness brought me the gift of a spiritual life that I have never before experienced. As it has turned out, my beliefs are not confined to one tradition over another. Our family was included in so many prayer and meditation groups from Christian traditions, to Jewish, to Buddhist, to Hindu, to the Cosmos to God. I was raised Christian, but could never quite connect my heart to the concepts put forth. It wasn't as though I didn't try. I felt punished when things went wrong, and the priests and pastors mostly reinforced this feeling when I confided in them. I felt no comfort and no sense that what was in my soul was any good. I thought that knowing the peace that is created by believing in the Divine would pass me by in this lifetime.

It was during an experience of Buddhist meditation that I began to realize and feel that what was deep inside of me was like a precious pearl: we were each put on this earth for a reason. "God doesn't give us anything we can't handle," began to make sense. The great mystical figures and their divinity no longer seemed so far removed. It has been such a special gift to feel that I have a cosmic and spiritual reason for being here, in this family, in this community, in this world. This closeness to God, or to my heart, has given me the feeling that it is right and good to try to help others, to rely on my intuitive nature, to be my God-given self. I am humbled, but I am also free. The quality of my relationships with my family, friends and clients reflect this, and I end up feeling grateful nearly every day.

Life has its ups and downs. It is neither bad nor good. It just is. Calamities come and go all the time. I think I understand them now more as opportunities than as punishment. The opportunities not to take ourselves, our families or our friends for granted present themselves in many ways. Just a few years ago, I wouldn't have imagined that I wouldn't be irritated by that phrase about light being at the end of the tunnel. I wouldn't have imagined that I would have been able to stop feeling like my problems were the center of the universe, to feeling completely sorry for myself and for my family. I really wouldn't have imagined that I would feel so enriched and grateful for having had the opportunity to live as this person in this time, in this place, and with my precious dear ones. I wouldn't have imagined I could love this much.

Getting Unstuck: How I Came to Spend a Life in Art

Lee Becker

Part of getting unstuck from an untenable situation is getting stuck in the first place: how I first became so stuck is a classically boring tale of events that led into a pregnancy at the age of sixteen and a marriage, which, in turn, became a struggle for existence. As it happened, my survival depended on one of the skills that is often employed by artists: to step back from a scene or situation and look at it as if from the viewpoint of a curious alien.

My stylish and well off parents adopted me from an agency in Kansas City, Missouri when I was six months old. My parents desperately wanted a child and I had been told by them and others in later years that "everyone" felt that a baby would make my new mother "straighten up." My father and his two brothers, all three with "movie-star good looks," had contracted the mumps while in their teens and had become sterile. My father, whose pride rested in his masculinity, could not admit to himself or to anyone else that he was deficient in this way and publicly blamed my mother for the lack of issue—one of many lies at her expense.

My parents' social life and business entertaining involved a great deal of drinking and partying and my mother had also become addicted to barbiturates as a remedy for lower back pain along with the booze.

Gradually our roles reversed: by the age of nine or ten I had become her mother, her guardian, her caregiver. My father divorced her and married his mistress, a jealous, grasping woman who managed to distance him from me, and tried to shut out his brothers and sister and his long time friends.

At different points there were things that helped me to take some control. One was a kind of "nervy-ness" that surfaced immediately after my first son was born. I took advantage of my family's rather exalted position in the conservative Kansas community in which I was, reluctantly, living, and became the first new mother to return to her high school after giving birth. This was in the 1950's, not exactly a time known for social enlightenment. Some parents of other students were outraged, some teachers reluctant but I had become disinterested in the traditional "joys" of high school activities and social life—at least those that were available to girls at the time.

My three sons were much loved. But, at the same, I felt trapped in an unrewarding marriage. My young husband was bi-polar. My mother's health was worsening. I was trying to shield my sons from the worst scenes and behaviors of her suicide attempts and her drinking bouts while trying to make them aware that these things exist in the world, and must be accommodated with compassion and understanding. I had begun to lose three days a week to migraine headaches and began to live on pain medication and the newly available Ritalin. Mother died at 56 of abdominal gangrene brought on by her assaults on her body...I was 26.

I hungered for an education. My father initially refused to help me financially to become a full time student. His view of the roles of women was a holdover from his father's era, and he insisted I should stay home and care for my family and if I got bored, should learn to play bridge or golf. During this time I was heavily engaged in reading and making drawings and paintings.

The realization that being adopted meant that I had none of the genetic material of these parents was one of the first revelations that gave me strength and some optimism. Another was acknowledging from the beginning that I was an artist, and drawing and painting kept my wits together. To be an artist means that one must look and look hard at one's surroundings and study and read and learn. One must learn to observe people, not to objectify them, which is a danger, but to understand as much as is possible about human nature. These observations are as important as the study of how to use line and form and color and space.

I read and learned about the natural world. I tried attending a church for a while and although I enjoyed the friendships that resulted, the rigid conventionalist viewpoints were too frustrating for me. I became involved with the civil rights, women's rights and the peace movements.

The house looked like it was going to the dogs (and literally, it was) but I was fighting back. I wanted to take my boys and leave, but I did not have a means to support them on my own, and didn't want to leave them in the hands of my husband's conservative relatives. After my mother died, I set out to get the education first, and I used some knowledge about my father's business practices to literally blackmail him. He paid my college expenses, and was surprised to find that I was a straight "A" student. I graduated with a degree in studio art and art education, took a smallish inheritance from a grandparent, and purchased a small ramshackle house in a neighboring town, a place where a sort of artists' community existed. The day I moved was the last day of migraine suffering. I still live there, and the condition of the house is what could be called, "stressed chic."

By this time my sons were either in college or working; I no longer needed to use Ritalin or painkillers. However, the worst blow was soon to come with the death of my youngest son, in a traffic accident. I came down with mononucleosis and could not work for a year. Friends helped me get through that very difficult period…a period which provided time to think.

I sorted out my feelings about my mother, realizing, as I had begun to understand earlier, she was more "sinned against than sinning." She was never mean or spiteful. And could be wickedly funny in her best moments. When I was still a child she had seen that I had any book I wanted and would defend my choices at the local library whenever the librarians were reluctant to let me take out what they considered improper choices. She encouraged my work in art.

My work began to get some attention. After a series of short-term teaching engagements, artist-in-residence gigs, making a modest living from my work, and with the help of friends, I finally felt that I had my life somewhat in my own hands. I have been given wonderful opportunities to travel to England and France, and most importantly, to India, a place which has long held a fascination for me, and still does. I've been able to work as a muralist in San Francisco and to spend additional time there, to just look and absorb and enjoy and work.

I finished graduate school and earned a Master of Fine Arts degree. I now teach part time in two small colleges and work on projects with an arts and humanities agency. My two surviving sons are working and relating with their worlds in their own unique ways and I'm very pleased with them both. Their father remarried, this time successfully.

In recent years there was another time of stress, this time a lack of cash. My stepmother had managed to entail most of my father's fortune away from all the adopted children and our legal attempts since her death have been costly and only somewhat successful. I tried Prozac during this time and did not like the flatness of emotions, so gave up on it, but it did ease the trauma of that year.

I am now grateful for the struggles. They contributed to the art that I do and gave me insight into the realities of peoples' private lives. I've enjoyed some meaningful relationships learning anew that what one sees on the surface of another is just that—a thin veneer to present to the world. I want my work to show what is under that veneer, at least give hints of the life within, no matter how surreal the life is or seems. I now give myself permission to live as I choose as much as possible and try to do as little harm as possible. The migraines have never returned.

Editors' note: We hope that you enjoy Lee's illustrations throughout this volume.

Seventeen Years Later: A Story for Jeffrey*

His tiny hands
Clenched thumbs wrapped by fingers too small to hold little else
Hold fast
His hair, dark and soft, brushes against my nose
It smells of new life
His body, naked against my chest—rising and falling like a boat in safe harbor—
Sleeps
Who has made this?
The trust of his quietude weighs more than he
How can so much love be so small?
Is God Jenny Craig? Does she think we can't handle larger portions?
I can not figure this out
So I sleep
My son's infant baby breaths mingle with my own
I approximate his mother
Knowing that in this moment
Of dream's ambered hue,
We hold each other
In God's warm,
Textured
Bliss

Jay Lappin
Previously published in *The Talking Stick4.99*

*The context for this piece was a writing workshop given by Katie Butler at the Networker Symposium. The assignment was to "write about something that gives you joy." I sat there among the quiet scribblings of the group and thought of the word *joy* to see what images would come up. What surfaced was a seventeen year old memory: my son sleeping on my chest when he was just weeks old. It was August, one of the hottest summers on record, and I was in the process of building my office on the back of my house. I had spent hours digging the foundation in the hard clay and had come into the house to take a break. The only semi-cool room we had was our bedroom. The air conditioner was huge, noisy, inefficient and looked like it had been manufactured in Edison's basement, but it was something. I came in, put the air on "High" and lay shirtless and exhausted on the bed. My wife, Joyce brought our new son in and lay him on my chest, saying something to the effect of, "you look like you could use some help." I lay there for awhile just looking at him—in full baby trance—and then I fell asleep. Joyce took our picture. Next month, Jeff turns 21. He's now 6' 1" and would crush me…

Three to Tango: She, He, and the Marriage

William Glasser as contributed by John Frykman[1]

Introduction: I use a method called structured reality therapy. It's focus is on what's good for a marriage, not on what may be good for one or the other partner

Script of the Approach with Jim and Bea

The way this works is, I'm going to ask you five questions. I'll try not to be harsh, but if I am, it's because I want to make sure you understand how important it is that you stick to the questions.

1. Are you here, Bea, are you here, Jim, because you want help with your marriage?

2. Whose behavior can you control? Jim? Bea?

3. Would each of you tell me what you believe is wrong with the marriage right now. This is your chance to complain.

4. In your opinion, what's good about your marriage right now?

5. This question is different from the others in the sense that it's less important that you try to figure out what I want. It's more important that you please each other. Tell me one thing that you, Bea, and you, Jim, could do all this coming week that you think will make your marriage better.

---

1.   Notes from a workshop by William Glasser, M.D. and Carleen Glasser—Evolution of Psychotherapy Conference at Anaheim, California, May 2000

If you are not both able to follow through, there's no need to have a second session.

Session Two

You're here, so I guess you followed through. How did it go?

Counseling is off to a good start, but there's still a lot to do. Like I said in the first session, if you can learn what's really going on here and use it, the counseling will never end.

BEA: What do you mean by that?

I'll show you. Each of you take a piece of this magic chalk. Draw a circle around both of you. It's called a solving circle. Keep in mind that the circle is only a chalk line; you can step out anytime you wish. I also call it a marriage circle. In it are a husband and wife; that's obvious. But there's another entity that's also in the circle. Can you think of what that entity could be?

JIM: It's our marriage.

That's right, and that's where the focus has to be to keep your marriage on track.

Get rid of the 'Seven Deadly Habits of Highly Miserable People.' These habits, if given enough time, will put an end to any relationship. They are: *criticizing, blaming, complaining, nagging, threatening, punishing,* and *bribing,* all ways in which we try to control other people.

Glasser closed the workshop by sharing with participants the book, 'Getting Together, Staying Together,' and offered the couple up to 20 follow up phone calls.

Bibliography

Glasser, W. (2000). *Counseling with choice theory.* New York, NY: Harper Collins.

Glasser, W. (1998). *Choice theory.* New York, NY: Harper Collins.

While You Sleep

Sitting at your bedside
Watching while you sleep
I find myself entering your body,
Slowly, carefully
not to disturb you
But to feel your pain,
Your agony,
your terror,
Of letting go
Of health and vitality.
They pour out of your body
Thrusting their way through your bowels
Under vehement protest of your merely mortal cries.

I massage your atrophying muscles
You watch your DNA, waiting for the fairies to repair the ladder.
We both see the platelets as they enter your bloodstream through the
    plastic
shunt
But neither if us can see how they steal away.
In all my fitness
I cannot stop the thief.

You stir
I must leave you now,
Trusting your indomitable spirit
To provide you with the strength you need
For your struggle to hold onto
Life itself.

Jeri Inger

Landing Gear

Douglas E. Doherty

July 10, 2003 Email from Doug to friends:

I guess Janice called some or all of you and mentioned something about a landing gear problem I had today. I don't know what was said, so I am taking a minute to inform you what happened.

Today around 10:00 am Alaska standard time I departed the village of Elim (Mike has been there!) Prior to raising my landing gear, I noticed in the mirror on the engine nacelle that the nose wheel (gear) had rotated a full 90 degrees from straight ahead! This is not common (never happened before) and not a good thing. I did not raise the landing gear because the nose wheel would not have fit into its place and may have been stuck up. I contacted the president, who was flying within radio range of me, and he asked me to fly to Kotzebue (Mike has been there too!!), about one hour away. We have maintenance there. Kotz is like Nome, they have full services, a hospital and everything. I had three adults, one child and a lapper (child under two) plus another pilot/mechanic that I was training. That makes seven souls.

I gained radio contact with our Kotz base and the mechanic on duty had his maintenance manuals standing by. The pilot I was training pulled out his Leatherman tool and started pulling access panels off the floorboard of the plane. We were trying to find the rudder/nose gear cable that broke, so we could pull on it ourselves to get the nose gear to straighten out for landing. It didn't happen, the cable had broken at the pedal and pulled itself through a bulkhead, out of sight and reach. Ok, now let's land! The problem with having the nose gear twisted sideways is that once it hits the ground, it may snap off, leaving you sliding on the props and the nose of the plane. The turbine engines on these planes cost well over $100,000 each and would be in need of total overhaul, if a prop contacts the ground. Another problem, the airplane might lurch to one side, sliding off the runway and into a nearby lake! The Kotz emergency response team was in place: several fire trucks, an ambulance and even a boat standing by for assistance.

At this pont I directed the pilot in training to assist the passengers and put them in the seats nearest the back of the plane. I gave him my thermos and anything else that I wouldn't want to get hit in the head with at 80 MPH! He secured these items. Runway closed (for me), I made my final approach. When I touched down, I had a modest audience: every soul on the airport was outside their respective hangers waiting for the smoke and fire. I landed smoothly on the mains, then tried to hold the nose off as long as possible to slow down as much as I could before losing control. If the plane was to start off to one side, I could use differential braking and differential reverse thrust to help aid in directional control. If the nose gear broke, then at least I would be going in a straight line! Because of all of the weight I had direct toward the back of the airplane, I was able to hold the nose up in the air for longer than I had anticipated. With all to see, I held the nose off, wheel twisted, for almost the entire—no pun intended—length of my roll out, rescue vehicles in chase! At the end, I lost aerodynamic control of my pitch axis (not enough wind over the elevator) and the nose wheel came gently down. Immediately upon touch down, the plane lurched to a stop with help from my right hand brake and some use of reverse.

I got another plane, loaded up my people and told them that there would be no additional charges for the extra flying!

End of story
Doug

Blows

Ben Furman

Food for Thought

- Why are people afraid of failing and 'botching up'?

- Is it right to always prepare yourself for the worst or should you expect things to go well?

- How should a good boss deal with mistakes that his subordinates make?

- Why do people sometimes seem capable of recovering from setbacks quickly and easily?

- How do other people's attitudes affect how capable a person is of getting over mishaps that he has suffered?

- What role does humour have when we look back over adversities that have happened in the past?

- Should we talk about our own botch-ups or is it better to keep them to ourselves?

- When things go wrong, what do you usually blame it on: circumstances or yourself or someone else?

- Sometimes it's necessary to study failures to find out exactly what caused them. Other failures should simply be put behind us and forgotten. How can we know which category a failure falls into?

- How can we help someone to get over failures as quickly as possible?

- How should we think if we want to be plagued by the memory of failures for a long time?

- What did Thomas Edison mean when he said that he had never failed?

- What is it that makes a hitchhiker able to carry on thumbing for a lift even though so many cars just drive past?

Relating to Setbacks, Failures, and Mistakes

Take a look at children as they learn how to do everyday things; to stand up, walk, talk, eat, get dressed, do a somersault, drink from a bottle, ride a bike, draw, and so on. When children are learning new skills, they fail all the time and make lots of mistakes. Most children cope with their mistakes in a very natural way; in other words, they hardly even notice them and just keep trying again. Some children, however, don't consider it such a trivial thing and fly into a rage every time they make a mistake. Take this example: Little Tina is trying to draw a circle, but it looks more like a pile of spaghetti than a circle. She examines the outcome and, unperturbed, takes another piece of paper to try again. Little Tommy, however, isn't exactly excited about drawing a circle, but decides to give it a try anyway. He doesn't make a very good job of it and can't make the ends of the circle join up with each other. He sees his failure, flies into a rage, scribbles all over the drawing, wailing, "I can't do it! I said I couldn't!" He then tears up the drawing and storms out, accidentally hitting other children with his flailing arms on the way. We adults, too, have our own ways of coping with the mistakes and botch-ups that we make.

Nine-year old William was chosen to be the goalkeeper in his new team. In the first game he let three goals in. Before the next game he went up to the coach and asked, "what can I do? There's no chance of me saving those kinds of balls again." The coach simply replied, "Don't even think about it, William. Just save one ball at a time." William wondered to himself what the coach might have meant. "What do you mean?" he asked, "There's only one ball on the field isn't there?" The coach replied, "all it means is that you mustn't think about anything except saving the next ball that flies towards the goal and then passing it to your team." William had an excellent match. He saved every ball and his team won the match. After the game, when his teammates were celebrating the victory, William ran out from his goal to the coach and asked, "who won, us or them?" He had been so committed to simply doing as his coach said and concentrating on the next thing that he didn't even know who had won.

In recent years, the term 'error-friendliness' has been adopted in scientific circles, and it simply means a positive attitude and approach towards mistakes. Error-friendliness epitomizes the idea that mistakes, blunders, and botch-ups can provide a key to learning, progress, and development, if people adopt a positive and genuinely interested attitude towards them. In actual fact, evolution is said to have been caused by nature's inclinations toward mistakes. Nowadays people in scientific research actively invest in mistakes and exploiting them.

Think back to a mistake or botch-up that you've made recently. How do you relate to it? Do you feel angry about it and regret it? Do you let it plague you? Are you still irritated about it? Is it possible that you've begun to see something positive in it? Could you even say that some good has come of your mistake? What good can you envisage coming from it in the long run? Has the mistake taught you anything positive? Could there be anything about your mistake that others, too, could benefit from?

How, then, do you relate to other people's mistakes? Do you often wonder how people can be so stupid or do you take a sympathetic and understanding attitude towards them? Do you say something like, "these things happen," or "it's good that it happened now so we know not to do it that way again…"?

Two rival shoe manufacturers in Finland both went to Africa at the same time to see whether or not it would be worth exporting shoes there. When the first arrived back home, his comment was, "what a wasted journey. Africans don't even wear shoes." When the second arrived home a few days later he greeted his family and colleagues enthusiastically, saying, "there sure is great market potential out there!"

Exercise

Make a note of all the setbacks that you've had in one week (your mistakes, unfortunate mishaps, failures, etc.) but make a conscious effort to face each setback that takes place with this mindset: Imagine that weeks, months or even years have passed and that you are in the future looking back at what has just happened. You recall the setback and remember that later on in your life it served some useful purpose. Either it taught you something useful or some good came as a result of it. Think of three good things that have come as a result of the setback and observe how these thoughts affect the way that you relate to that setback now.

Relating to Others' Setbacks, Failures and Mistakes

When other people tell you about the setbacks they've suffered it's usually because they want to know what you think about what happened to them. By choosing your words carefully, you can encourage them to get over the setback. If you don't think about what you say you'll only be doing them a disservice and will only increase the likelihood of them being plagued by the incident for longer.

Perhaps the best starting point for understanding how best to help someone who has undergone setbacks is to first imagine what you could say in a situation if you wanted to make someone feel worse about the incident for longer. Here's how it works:

Make it clear you're not interested about what happened
"Sorry, I've got to go—I'm in a bit of a hurry."
"I couldn't care less."
"You'll never guess what happened to me once..!"

Dismiss the incident
"Oh that's nothing at all, really."
"That's nothing compared to what happened to so-and-so!"
"That happens to everyone at some point."
"You've got to take the rough with the smooth."

Criticize the person for the way he relates to the incident
"You're making a mountain out of a molehill."
"You're taking this a bit seriously, aren't you?"
"Why go and blow a little thing like that right out of proportion?"
"That happens to everyone, so it's not even worth thinking about."

Act surprised that the person is still bothered by the incident
"And you're still bothered about that?"
"Are you intending to spend the rest of your life worrying about it?"
"Why can't you just put it behind you?"
"Are you still crying over spilt milk?"

If you want to guarantee that someone will continue being bothered by something, that's the way to go about achieving it. If, however, you want to be of assistance to someone and really help them get over something quickly you should do exactly the opposite. In other words:

Show that you're interested and listen
"Please do tell me."
"Would you mind telling me more...?"
"Really? Please do explain!"

Acknowledge the emotional gravity of the incident
"It's terrible for something like that to happen."

"That would really bug me, too."
"Anyone would feel bad if that happened to them."

Compliment the person for the way they relate to the incident
"I have to take my hat off to you for staying so calm about it."
"I'm sure I'd have blown my top by now!"
"How on earth did you manage to make things work out so well despite all that?"

Show you understand that the incident might take a while to get over
"It would take anyone a fair amount of time to get over that."
"It's good that you can talk about it."

In other words, if you want to help people who share with you that things have gone badly for them or that something they've done has gone wrong, don't reproach them for the way they react to the incident, but instead, support their emotional reaction. Show them that you fully understand that it's hard for them to get over the incident. You could, perhaps, say that if the same thing had happened to you it would be hard for you to get over it, too. Also, encourage the way that they relate to the incident and only later sit down with them to think about how they could put the incident behind them as painlessly as possible.

In Search of Tikkun Olam After September 11, 2001[1]

Oh eternal Source of life
Source of what connects everyone and everything
And of what disconnects:

I don't know that I can call you God
Or Adonai Eloheinu, Allah, the Tao
Or any other name for all that connects,
That makes meaning
Or that people use to separate themselves
In Your name.

But today, in my grief
I must reach out to Your one-ness
To Your many-ness
To all that exists,
Which is You, Which is us, Which is everything
All connected.
We are of you, of the universe
But we forget.
Which explains my tears today.

In this time of grief and of fear
Too great to describe in my meager words
I call out for healing to the rhythms of universal connection

---

1.   *The Hebrew "Tikkun Olam" refers to the spiritual obligation to mend a broken world

26

To the ground and to the air and to the waters that sustain me and all
    who live
To the stars and planets as you vibrate in harmonies I cannot
    understand
To the leaves, hinting of autumn glory
To every tender exchange ever shared between people and peoples.
I call out:

Oh Oneness oh Many-ness
Please help me find strength
With so many dead to grieve at once.
Not the strength to make others afraid
Not the strength to make revenge
Not the strength to continue this cycle of evil.
That is no strength to me
But only fear and pain and righteous anger transformed,
Desecrated, perverted, without healing.

Oh Source of life
Oh One-ness proliferating into Many-ness
Oh Many-ness unifying the harmonies of the Universe
Oh music of stars and quarks and birds and whales
And music of many rituals observed around the world:

This is the help I ask.
To find the strength to love through my tears and my fears
To love all the dead of this dreadful time
To love all who love each and every one of them.
It's not hard to love the passengers and crew,
Fashioned against their will into tools of others' destruction.
Not hard to love the cleaning women and businesspeople.
Easy to love heroic rescuers caught in the inferno
Crushed below so many stories so many lives.

Not hard to love those who will never stop yearning
For their loved ones' return, never to be.

But how can I find the strength
To love the assassins? I said Kaddish for them too.
But I know that is not enough.
What anguish brought them to this terrible place?
Can I love their mothers and their orphaned sons,
Some of whom will take their place
Some of whom will work for peace?
This is hard, so hard, but I must.
My world, perhaps something even greater
Depends on it.

Can I love the Palestinian boy, my cousin,
Rock in hand?
Yes I can. He is a child and I love him.
But can I love the Israeli soldier who guns him down?
Can I love this child's brother,
Who waits three years to take his revenge
On a bus filled with Jews?
Can I love an Israeli government who forgets
That we too once were strangers
Blamed for all wrong with the world?
This is hard, so hard, but I must.
My world, perhaps something even greater
Depends on it.

Can I love those who believe the Taliban

Crusher of women
Perverter of Islam
Will root out evil
And who are willing to die
To avenge American bombings on Arab soil?

This is hard, so hard, but I must.
My world, perhaps something even greater
Depends on it.

Can I cry enough for half a million Iraqi children
Or for my own government whose righteousness
Caused their deaths by blockade?
No milk, no penicillin, no compassion from the powerful.
Can I care enough about why so many people hate my beloved home
And stop the bombings stop the despoiling
Of Your beautiful and damaged earth?
This is hard, so hard, but I must.
My world, perhaps something even greater
Depends on it.

Oh Source of life and of all the connections in the universe
Can I care enough about the despoilers of the earth,
The greedy so despised and feared,
To help them to help us to help me
Know that we create our own destruction
With every soul we ignore
With every soul we reject
With every soul we hurt
With every person and every thing we use up
And throw away?

Oh eternal Source of connection and disconnection,
Of life, of peace,
Of death and of hatred
Help me.
Help me find the only strength that matters.
Oh One-ness and Many-ness
We may call you Adonai Eloheinu
or Allah or the Tao or we may call you many gods.
Or we may not call you at all.

Whatever we imagine to be true
Please, please
Give me the strength to help grow compassion for all
And to grow enough compassion to go around
     and around

     and around.

How else to heal a shattered world?
How else to do Tikkun Olam?
How else to heal myself?

Jodie Kliman
September 18, 2001/Rosh Hashana, 5762

How Not to Get Stuck by Calamity: "High Flight"[1]

Joellyn L. Ross

July, 1998. I remember him half-sitting, half laying on the couch in the screened-in porch, wearing jeans and a striped polo shirt, looking very thin and wan, maybe in pain; he wouldn't say. "You know," he said, "how I feel now is the best I'll ever feel…and that's not too good."

My father was dying from lung cancer and still trying to look at life objectively, observing himself as dispassionately as possible. He'd fought the illness hard: at diagnosis, four years ago, he'd been given a prognosis of only 18 months. But he knew he had to stay alive for his and my mother's 50th wedding anniversary, which they observed in March, 1998. Now he had one more goal: attending his Air Force reunion in August. "My last hurrah," he said.

He and my mother made it to the reunion—barely, with my father stubbornly driving the five hours each way, my mother gritting her teeth the whole time. Thankfully, Air Force buddies kindly hovered during the entire reunion, helping father, who, by that time, was very weak.

Dad contacted Hospice when they got home. He put his characteristic upbeat spin on it when he told me, "There's only a couple hospice centers in the state, and one of them—brand new—is only fifteen minutes away. It's beautiful, first class," he said.

I flew out to Ohio about a week after my father had begun the hospice program. It was shocking to see him sitting in the family room in his favorite chair, hooked up to an oxygen tank, looking very frail and sick. His mood, however, belied his condition. He raved about the hospice center and is amenities, and urged my mother to take me there to see it as soon as possible.

---

1. "High Flight" is the name of the Air Force Hymn, which was the closing song at my father's memorial service.

How to cope with calamity? It helps to be born, like my father, with the temperamental inclination to make gourmet lemonade from that dozen lemons sent your way. "I'm making my final approach said my father, Dwight Ross. Once he'd decided death was inevitable, he went into lemonade making with a vengeance.

There was, for example, his obituary. He wrote up a draft, then insisted that I work on it with him. I approached it like any other editing project, being rather hardnosed with my suggestions and corrections.

He was fine with that. We argued over the correct wording, the order in which life events should go, which relatives to mention, and so forth. I typed up several drafts which we mailed back and forth until he approved the final version. He seemed utterly pleased to have his life represented in a way that he found both honest and flattering. And to have written it himself.

Planning his memorial service was another task he approached with enthusiasm, saying, "It's the last party I'll ever get to plan, and I'm the star." He didn't want a funeral—"too depressing"—so he and my mother agreed that burial would be family-only, followed by a more public memorial service at their church. He sat in the family room with a notepad on his lap, writing up the agenda he wanted for his final "party." He didn't want any sad music and was especially pleased when the church organist said he'd play "Just a Closer Walk with Thee" and the other hymns at a hearty gospel tempo. The organist also agreed to play the Air Force Hymn as a closing, something very important to my father, who was rightfully proud of his achievements during WWII service.

My father wasn't a big talker, especially about emotions. We didn't have in-depth discussions, yet he and I had a strong connection; we understood each other at a deep, visceral level, and we knew we had it. Nevertheless, the psychologist in me prompted me, at one point, to say to my father that, given the circumstances, perhaps we should have "the talk" that people are supposed to have with dying loved ones. He gave me a wry look, then said with a twinkle in his eye, "okay…but let me get my list…." I laughed, he laughed, and that was our version of "the talk."

I know there was genuine sadness behind all my father's "spin doctoring" about his final days. During the years of his illness, he expressed many times that he was surprised that this had happened to him. He had counted on living until he was 84, and he was going to die at 77. He loved his life, his wife, his children, and his home. He was proud of his achievements. He didn't want to leave it all. His illness and impending death were a calamity for him, for all of us.

Looking back, being with my father while he was dying had a surreal quality to it, which, I now reflect, likely was the effect from coupling hyper-realism with a strong undercurrent of deep sadness denied. At the time, however, I joined him in his positive attitude and sunny outlook about his life and its impending end; was it for his benefit or mine or all of ours? Despite the surrealistic quality to his cheerfulness, it did allow all of us, however weirdly, to talk about what was going on. My father said, many times, to each of us, how much he loved us, how proud of us he was, and how pleased he was with how his life turned out and that he had no regrets. He actively, in his own way, provoked closure. For this, I am very, very grateful.

How to get unstuck from catastrophe? The lesson my father taught me was not to let calamity stick you. His working philosophy was: make the best of it, deal with it head-on, and don't whine. I admired his rationality and stoicism, and his example has helped me deal with my own calamities throughout my life. I'm glad that, thanks to him, my first impulse is to stay dispassionate until I have a chance to size up the situation.

The day before my father died, I called the hospice center to check on his condition. The nurse said, in the most euphemistic way, that he was near death. "You're getting ready to land, Dad," I said to myself and smiled, knowing that was exactly how he would want me to think about it.

Unstuck and Set Free

Joan Barth

High Technology is a puzzle to me. But I am willing to learn more about it. This is a story of a family's getting unstuck with the help of technology.

When a man phoned to set up an appointment for his far-flung siblings to meet and discuss the past, I was reluctant but interested. The telephoning brother promised to do all the background work. All I had to do was to collect the emails of each sibling's version of the past. I figured I could do that. I agreed to see the family on a Saturday for six hours. The eight siblings would arrange to converge on my little town from Texas, Mexico, California, Europe, India, and nearby Pennsylvania towns at the appointed time. The answer to whom had recommended me was the Internet. I am a clinical member of AAMFT and the Directory lists all clinical members.

After making an appointment time, each of the family siblings sent me an email telling me their version of their years at home. I made notes in the margins as I read them after saving them to my computer.

When the appointed time came, I had read eight emails that gave different stories of the past and different emphases on events that had happened. The major reason for meeting was that one sister was having much difficulty about sexual abuse—abuse that they had all experienced in some way.

One sister, Marion, had driven alone from nearby. She was the first to arrive. She made it very clear that she was there for her sister, Clotilde's, sake. She said there was nothing wrong with her. The others came to my office in two cars, having met at the caller's house first. They arrived together. The family made a lot of small talk about my office while they took their seats.

I began the session by asking if it was okay to audiotape it and telling them the schedule. We would meet for three hours, have a two hour lunch break and meet again for three hours.

I distributed throws and a quilt for those who had come from warm locations. I told them where restaurants were and where the bathroom and microwave were. I asked if anyone smoked. Only Marion did. I asked who would be responsible for paying me and that I would accept payment after lunch. Finally, I gave each of them two index cards and a pencil. I asked that they write on each card what three goals they wanted to accomplish in our time

together. They could keep one card and give the other to me. They would never show the card to their siblings—it would be private information.

I started by saying how fearful I was of dealing with this family. I told them I had discovered through their emails that when any of them was angry with another, it might be years before they spoke to that person again. I did not want to be the cause of such estrangement. So I felt unfree to do my usual family therapy. After being assured that I could say whatever I wanted or ask what I believed to be appropriate, I continued.

First of all, I commended them for being willing to come so far to help their sister. Not all families would do such a thing, I noted. Neither the sister who had requested the meeting, Clotilde, nor her siblings was able to validate my commendation.

I also commended them for using email to portray to me their rendition of how their family interacted. Again they demonstrated a lack of energy towards my commendation. Then I asked them how they had demonstrated their gratitude to Martin for all the work he had done in setting up the meeting. Martin, a cancer patient, was obviously working very hard to sit comfortably in his chair. He kept squirming around and put his hands under his chair on the bag that held his bandages and medication. But Martin didn't want to be commended either. Nor was there much discussion when I asked how they were dealing with his illness and possible death.

We began to discuss their present relationships with their parents. None of them had kept in touch with their father but they all were in contact with their mother who lived in Mexico, where they all were born and brought up. They telephoned her at least once a week and some called her every day.

Each of them sends money to their mother monthly. None of their spouses objects. The mother refuses to leave her home or make arrangements for herself when she will be unable to maintain herself there. She says she will not take the father back unless he is sick or in need. As usual, when things do not require current fixing, the family does nothing to plan for the future.

The family, in their first three hours, touched on their abuse. Each of them had been sexually abused by cousins but did not enlist one another or either of their parents to help them with that problem. Because their parents set up a life that centered on themselves, not their children, the children do not feel important to them. They deny any anger because of their insignificance. Yet they feel vindicated that their parents are unhappy now. I pointed out how the children did not use resources when they were young but they use them as adults. They use their siblings, spouses, and professionals now. However, they continue to keep their parents out of the loop. I felt it important to articulate what was never said in the family.

After three hours, we broke for lunch. All of the siblings waited while Martin took his medication and changed his bandage. Again high tech aided our meeting. Years ago, someone with intestinal cancer would have been unable to be part of such a session.

The first thing Martin did after lunch was give me payment for the six hours. He had collected the money from his siblings to pay me during lunch, a lunch they shared with one another.

I then asked the group members to take out their index cards. It was important that they get what they wanted from the session. I told them that if they hadn't gotten their three goals, they had three hours to make certain they did. Some of them had reached none of their goals. I shared with them that I always set up goals before going to an event. I usually meet my expectations.

In the final three hours, Clotilde told the entire story of how she had been sexually abused. She said that her father had told a friend he was excited by his daughter. Marion, the first arrival, brought up that she was sorry for telling the mother that the youngest son, Howard, was homosexual, despite the fact that Howard had not become open about his homosexuality. She admitted that she did so as revenge because Howard had abused her college-age son. Howard had called the son to apologize and they had worked out their problem. Marion said she never wanted to speak to Howard again. The siblings got very tense when she said this. Howard openly told what he had done and said he was very wrong. He went into the specifics about being turned on by his nephew and inviting him into an empty bedroom where they had sex. Again he said he was wrong.

At that time, we took a smoking and bathroom break.

When we reassembled, Marion began to apologize: "When I went out on the balcony to smoke, I realized that there was nothing more Howard can do. I must forgive him. And I do."

She turned to her brother.

"Howard, I am very sorry to have caused you pain."

They got up, walked across the room, and hugged.

After we talked further, Mark asked me if this was therapy. It seemed so casual to him. He expected therapy to be more studied. Despite that, he was meeting his goal which was "better communication among us without fear of separation."

The sister who wanted help put her head down and closed her eyes when her siblings asked her questions about her abuse. They didn't ask her specific questions but rather allowed her to be very abstract. It became clear that this family assumed much without getting pertinent data to back up their feelings. I made it clear to them that they had very little to corroborate their anger. That fact became more and more apparent to each of them as they spent additional time with their brothers and sisters.

I told Clotilde that when we close our eyes we relive the past instead of being in the present. I also let all of them know I had set up a teleconference a month later for them to discuss any issues that arose because of our session. I gave each of them the "bridge" number where we could meet. Then they left laughing and hugging. They had become unstuck.

Each of the siblings emailed me that the follow-up session on the Bridge was unnecessary. They were keeping in touch by the use of high tech.

Some while later, Clotilde called me to say Martin, the 42 year old brother who had set up the meeting, was on his deathbed. All the siblings had convened to be with him.

Walls

Far simpler to let the walls around me be.
Walls protect and defend.
They salve expectation
Make things stark and clear.

I don't hurt if I do not risk.
I just feel trapped
Like a blade of May grass
Pinned between concrete cracks
Choked by tar.
I see pitch black instead of
Moving grey mist.
Black, like darkness, lets me sleep.

But I am drawn to moving grey.
Grey pierces walls, wrenches the core.
Grey attracts,
Stuns me with confusion,
Bottoms me out for lack of framework.
Grey makes me shiver and move.

It is the pain of movement that draws.
The exhilaration of risk,
Wanting to know what I do not yet.
Wanting me instead of my walls.

Walls protect
Yet hold me prisoner inside.

Kathleen C. Laundy

Bundles

There was a time you needed bundles,
Souvenirs of home to comfort
Touch tokens to soothe,
Mementos to shelter you
From world fears and soul threats.
Now you stand at the door
Ready to launch, radiant.
Naked of things
Armored in spirit.
You prepare for the journey
To your next lighting place.
I notice how small your bundles now are.
And I marvel.
You now carry
Home
Inside you.

Kathleen C. Laundy

You Forgot the Cookies

Home cookies were meant to soothe you
When your world was cold
When we weren't there to nurture
When you felt alone.

They were symbols of connection
How food makes you grow
How baking warms the heart
Nourishes the soul.

Now you know.
You bake for yourself
And give kitchen gifts to others.
I am moved with wonder.

At the life you are living.
The warmth you are giving
And your power to remember
Childhood's love as you sample the adult.

When you left, you forgot my home cookies.
I taste their bittersweet.
Flavor echoes both rich delight
In your growth.

And the pain
Of giving witness
To the passage
Of your childhood.

Kathleen C. Laundy

Mamma

"Mamma, Mamma," she calls.

    "Mamma, Mamma, and Mamma again.
    The soothing chant of mother sounds,
    Naming her first mentor-muse.

"Mamma!" she demands.

    Watch.
    Witness her first giant steps
    Starting, stumbling towards womanhood.

"Mamma!" she retorts.

    Righteous.
    Anger drives her lurching towards definition
    As separate, unique
Whole.

"Mamma?" she implores.

    Tears, overcome by wonder-worry
    Of new motherhood.
    Umbilical folds pulsing,
    Enveloping them all.

"Mamma!" she celebrates.

    Toast to life goals met.
    To starts and stalls

To the bittersweet
Of memory making.

"Mamma…" she grieves.

Witness to diminishing life
Prone and brittle before her.
Ebbing, ebbing.
Umbilical wrenched.

Kathleen C. Laundy

Dreaming About Solutions

Terry Soo-Hoo

Kathy woke up in a cold sweat, her heart pounding. Something was squeezing her chest, making it hard for her to breathe. As she gasped for breath she suddenly realized it was only a dream! It was a terrible nightmare but it really didn't happen. Thank God, she said to herself. Her dream was so real! In her dream, it was a very stormy, windy, and rainy night. They were driving home. They began to have one of their usual arguments. The argument kept escalating and escalating, until they were yelling at each other with ear piercing volume. Suddenly her husband lost control of the car on a slippery part of the winding road. Her husband slammed on the brakes. With the cry of screeching tires, he drove off the road, right through the railing, and struck a tree 50 feet away. She somehow managed to survive the crash, but her husband did not. Dazed and disoriented she desperately climbed out of the car. She turned around to look at the demolished car with her husband still inside and started to scream. Then the shock, grief, intense pain, and sense of terrible loss overcame her. But it was only a dream. Her husband was still sleeping next to her. His loud snores were oddly reassuring. Maybe her unconscious was trying to tell her something? Now everything that her marriage counselor had said to her last week came rushing through her mind.

"It is very common for loving people to find themselves slipping into painful and unsatisfying ways of relating to each other. Very often each person in the relationship has been emotionally injured from many years of painful interactions. So what is needed are healing ways to bring both people back to together, to bring back the love and caring that often gets forgotten or put aside in the struggles and conflicts that go on in a troubled relationship."

Kathy had thought at the time that he made a lot of sense. But she was reluctant to do any of the things the counselor suggested because she was still so angry with her husband and could not let go of the anger. As her heart slowly stopped pounding and returned to normal, she realized in a shock that something was more important than the anger, and that was saving her marriage. She heard the counselor say:

"Solving this problem will not be easy. It will require a lot of courage, strength, tolerance, intelligence and most of all, love for each other and your family. Do you feel up to the challenge?"

She knew now that it was true, they both had to put aside their anger and resentments and work together to solve the problems in their marriage. Now, what did he say about this "Finding Solutions Plan"? The counselor's words rang in her head.

"This plan will require that both of you do things that are different from how you have been behaving. First you will need to pause and observe what is happening in your relationship. To be a good observer is an excellent skill to have. It requires patience, insight, intelligence, self-control, and inner strength. Most of all, it will require that you be able to disengage from the intensity of the emotions at the moment, in essence to be 'objective.' If either one gets drawn into a verbal argument or disagreement and get too emotional during this observation period, you need to physically leave the verbal argument if possible and calm yourselves down."

That's it, she thought, we'll do it. We'll carry out the steps. Now what did he say about the steps? How do problems start? And how do they get escalated? What works and what does not work? Kathy thought to herself, arguments often start when I get upset at how my husband comes home and ignores me. I'm really stressed out and he doesn't care.

I usually get mad and tell him how inconsiderate he is and how he never shows any interest in me any more, why did he even marry me. This usually has the effect of causing him to yell back about how I am such a nag and stop harassing him. This doesn't work very well. When I remain calm and less emotional that works better.

I can see that both of us are so caught up in a power struggle over who is right and who is wrong, as well as who needs to change first. And we are caught in non-productive arguments that lead nowhere and just make us more angry and frustrated. Both of us are hyper-sensitive to each other and are over reacting to even little things. Also both of us are angry, hurt, and vulnerable due to past negative events that have happened to us.

Now, what did the counselor say about healing the hurt feelings that have been building for so long?

"Both of you will come up with two things that will represent 'healing gestures.' These two healing gestures will say: 'I am ready to work on healing our hurt feelings and bringing us back together again as a couple and as a family.' Do not tell each other what you did as the two healing gestures. Each person will guess as to what these gestures are and come back next time to report. We will see how accurate your guesses are."

It had been a very stressful week and Kathy had gotten very little sleep. So as she struggled to remember the counseling session it was harder and harder to concentrate. Her mind was slowing down and she was getting tired and drowsy. She woke up in a jolt and realized that she had fallen asleep again. She checked her heart and breathing. This time her heart was OK, not pounding. The pressure on her chest had lessened a lot. Her breathing was OK, she wasn't panting or grasping for air. Then she realized she had another dream. This time she dreamed that she had actually carried out the counselor's homework assignment and it felt good. Furthermore, she had dreamed that her husband had also carried out the assignment as well. In her dream she was saying:

"I think that I was watching for Robert's 'healing gestures' so much that I kept seeing how he does in fact do a lot of things for me, like washing the dishes, getting me my special ice cream, fixing my car, and so on. One day he came home with my special favorite perfume! You can't imagine how that floored me, what a surprise!"

Her husband also was reporting to the counselor his progress: "When I focused on looking for Katy's healing gestures, I also saw a lot of things Kathy was doing for me that I didn't noticed before, like cooking my favorite foods, washing my clothes, taking care of all the little things around the house. There is a DVD player I had wanted to buy. But I was holding off because I did not know how she would react. One day she brought home the DVD player and said it would be nice to watch some good movies together. We had not just stayed home and watched a good movie together for a long time. We even sat on the sofa and cuddled. I liked that."

How strange, is this how counseling supposed to work? I do all these things in my dreams and somehow my problems are supposed to be solved? Kathy began to get drowsy again. As she drifted off, she continued to hear the counselor's voice in her head.

"The next step in healing this relationship is to have each of you generate even more special ways of helping each other. I want each of you to think about this question: Kathy in what ways does your husband need you? And Robert in what ways does your wife need you?"

She heard herself say: "I think my husband really needs help to organize things better. He is very sloppy and inefficient. He can't remember his appointments. He has trouble paying attention to the details and forgets a lot of things."

She heard her husband say: "My wife could use help in calming down, be less uptight, and more relaxed. She worries all the time about even very small things. She is a worry wart. I am concerned that she will get a heart attack or an ulcer from worrying. Her anxiety and worrying sometimes has bad effects on the kids as well."

"The next assignment is for each of you to work out a way to help the other on these specific areas. The conditions are that each of you must do this in a supportive way and without criticism and feelings that one person is bossing the other around."

As Kathy felt the sleepy dreamy state overtake her again, her last thoughts were about how her mother was having another medical crisis and was probably going to be hospitalized soon. This was really creating a great deal of stress for her. She thought through her dreamy haze that if only her husband could support her through this ordeal instead of calling her "crazy" or "control freak."

Kathy was no longer clear if she was dreaming or awake. Maybe she was in between the waking and dream worlds. She heard herself say: "Last few weeks have been much improved. We are not arguing and fighting as much now. I feel that Robert has really tried to show he cares about me and I appreciate his efforts. My mother had a medical crisis a few weeks ago and I have been very stressed out. Robert has been very supportive and has helped me keep from going crazy with worry. In the past he would have gotten upset with me when he saw how worried I was. He would have yelled at me to stop worrying or to snap out of it. He would say that my hyper-anxiety was upsetting the kids. This last couple of weeks when he saw I was stressed out with worry he just hugged me. He didn't have to say a word. I just felt that he was there for me. It reminded me of when we were dating, how he would just hold me in his arms and how good it felt."

Then she heard her husband say: "I agree that the last few weeks have been much better. I feel Kathy has not been down on me with the usual criticism and nagging. When Kathy's mother fell ill, I felt that she reached out to me and let me support her and help her cope with the stress. In the past she would have taken out her stress on me. This time I really felt needed and appreciated.

"She also made a list of a few things she wanted me to do around the house. This time instead of making it seem like I had to do them or else I was a no good lazy bum, she kissed the note with her lipstick lips and wrote, "Thanks for helping out." This made me feel like she appreciated my help. She helped me remember things by making a list of times and dates for events and appointments, like when we were scheduled to go to the annual company dinner. She also kissed this list. Every time I saw that lipstick kiss on the note I smiled. She used to do that when we were dating."

She felt her body relaxing and letting go of years of painful tension. The pressure in her chest was completely gone. There was warmth in her chest and a pleasant glow around her face that she had not noticed before. The counselor was saying something important so she strained to hear him.

"I am impressed with how the two of you have been able to reach out to each other and change the way you were relating. It seems like you guys have found different ways of helping and supporting each other.

Kathy suddenly woke up. The sun was shining brightly through the window, filling the bedroom with a warm glow, illuminating up her chest and face. The window was open and she could hear the birds singing to each other in the backyard. Funny how she didn't noticed them before. It was 8 am Sunday morning, and despite all the dreams she had during the night she felt energized. She looked over at her husband sleeping soundly next to her and was filled with so many emotions. She gently placed her head on his chest and listened to his rhythmic breathing. He slowly placed his arm about her. Was he awake or asleep? Could he be having the same dreams? Then through the stillness he whispered, "I love you." She smiled. Somehow she knew it was going to be a good day.

My Discovery of Transition

Murray Korngold

In the fifty years that I've spent doing psychotherapy and counseling, nothing has been as useful to me as my own experiences of difficult life transitions. On a number of occasions in childhood, adolescence, and maturity I've had the sense of being stuck in a doorway.

At the age of twelve I was a somewhat solitary and dreamy boy who had yet to bond with other boys. I loved reading, listening to music and roller skating to the city limits of Detroit, which in 1932 was only a small fraction of the size that Detroit is today. Although I had been a frail fellow, given to long bouts of illness, I don't recall having been fearful or anxious about anything in particular. I was being reared by a single parent, my mother, who worked six days a week literally from dawn till dusk and was looked after by a host of relatives, her six married siblings and her parents. I wandered, as I recall, in a relatively carefree manner around this tribe of orthodox Jewish immigrants, who disapproved of my feckless ways but who fed me and saw to my needs nonetheless.

I can't recall, precisely, what triggered the horror that I lived with for months, but at some point I realized that I would die, that I was not immortal. Perhaps it was the spectacle of a small animal, a cat or a dog being accidentally killed. I'm not certain, but like a thunderclap out of a cloudless sky, came this sudden realization that I could die at any moment and that that would be the end of me. It was difficult for me to think for very long about anything else. For the first time, I feared the dark and began to fight with frugal relatives who insisted that I turn the lights out when I went to sleep. I purchased a flashlight which I kept under my pillow so that I would never have to be in the dark. Moreover, I resisted falling asleep for fear that I would die in my sleep, unknowingly. Inevitably, of course, I would fall asleep but would wake frequently during the night to see if I were still alive.

What disturbed me most of all was my sense of utter isolation, because, despite my intuitive sense that discussing this was futile, I couldn't help myself: I simply had to inquire into why it was that my uncles, aunts and cousins weren't as terrified as I was. I would have dreams in which many of those whom I knew and liked were being eaten alive by wild beasts while I, cowering in a closet, weeping and shaking with terror, could not understand why no one else was hiding. I asked the people I respected the most why they weren't afraid and got answers which to my mind (I was already an atheist and a devotee of scientific thought) were monstrously foolish, absurd.

These answers had to do with God's plan, the way things are and that it was, anyway, silly for a young child to think of such things. Some teachers would answer with philosophical meanderings that to me were incomprehensible. How could they all be so tranquil when their pants were on fire? What was wrong with everybody? I went to the library and read tracts on Zionism, Communism, mysticism, practically all of which were simply gobbledygook. I took home the Bible in the English language, read Ecclesiastes secretly on the porch and cried hopelessly. There was no good news anywhere. Every now and then I would encounter a grown-up who looked intelligent and would broach the inevitable question. Even now I marvel at the fact that I don't recall a single person who reported feeling fear or for that matter who even took the question seriously. I don't know how many months this lasted. It could have been a few months or more than a few. On dark nights I would occasionally walk alone down the middle of a dark rat-infested alley to see if I could exorcize the fear that way, but these efforts only made me more fearful and obsessed. It was an insatiable itch. I couldn't stop scratching.

I lost weight, ate and slept poorly. My relatives complained about my eccentricities to my mother who, in her careless rapture of habitual denial, would pooh-pooh their complaints. I tried taking up activities to distract myself and I remember the precise moment when it all resolved. I had become interested in the Boy Scout movement and also had become enchanted by geometry. One Saturday morning I took a bus to Palmer Park where tests for merit badges were being given to tenderfoot scouts to advance them to the rank of second class scouts. I built a campfire, alternately walked and jogged a mile in 12 minutes, read a compass and a map, identified a number of trees, and was advanced to the status of second class scout. Flushed with triumph, I headed out to the bus stop to go home, but, as it was a lovely, mild afternoon decided to lie on the grass and look up at the clouds. As soon as I did, the Question appeared. How can I bear it, that I'm going to die? It's not fair. It's awful, that I should cease to exist and that the joyous hubbub of life and fun was going to go on without me. At that moment, something different occurred. An invisible interlocutor asked me in a quiet Socratic manner or perhaps in a very sensible Euclidian manner, "what exactly about not existing bothers you so much?" And I answered, "what bothers me is that I will be non-existent for an infinite time, for ever and ever." And the interlocutor went on, "but isn't it the case that before your birth you non-existed for an infinite time for ever and ever?"

Mind you I had simply assumed that the universe had existed for ever and ever. This was long before I had heard of the Big Bang theory, so I agreed, "yes, that's true." The interlocutor continued, "So, are you afraid of the infinite time of nonexistence before your birth?" "No," I answered, not quite knowing where the interlocutor was going with all this, although the hair was beginning to stand up on the back of my neck. "Well, then, if it's true that things which are equal to the same thing are equal to each other, then aren't the two infinite non-existences identical?"

I felt as if I were being tutored and being led by the hand, step by step, in a direction that was irresistible. "So," I said, "They're identical. So then what?" "Well, that means you're afraid of one of them, but not of the other. You should either be afraid of both of them, or afraid of neither of them, right?" That really stopped me in my tracks. The beauty of it, the elegance of it delighted me. My spirits rose like a helium-filled balloon and I instantly realized what the Greek ancient, Zeno had said, "death means nothing to me for when death is, I am not and when I am death is not." And for a wonder, although almost 70 years have gone by since that magical realization, I have never feared death. Paradoxically, although I am not so certain now as I was then that nothing continues after biological death—I am mystically agnostic—death still has no terrors for me. My first route for surrender to reality was the route of rational thought. Since then I have found other routes. But it always does begin with a direct experience of acceptance.

Kaddish for My Father

Joel Carroll, born Joseph Cohen
(after Allen Ginsberg)

Strange I should go to New York this October night,
walk down the Boulevards of Brooklyn
to a wedding on your side of the family
while Manhattan's million incandescent eyes shine,
and I used to think they were stars.

Bob Dylan's new CD scratches in the back—
how the legends fade—hollow eyes not yet closed
as the year plays out. Escape to oblivion's no more
an option—life in L.A., worshiping green.
The real estate market stirs and takes a turn—
appetites whet—I raise my rates.
The caissons must be dug six feet deeper,
and my bill's been raised by one hundred percent.

Strange how potato eyes grow under the Tennessee sky
and sprout as some rooted thing does—
you could no longer live on Long Island,
and I salute you.

The red-eye I take on Saturday night descends
into Kennedy. I walk the cobblestone Bowery streets—
bums asleep in doorways—the homeless wasn't
even invented back when we went to The Cooper Union
until I found I hadn't the stomach for it.
Shooting pool at Julian's off Union Square—

we looked at Brunswick-Balke slate tables—three-inch
thick slabs—enough for a man the size of you—
me not yet a big apple.

Love is a fragile thing—dissolved in tears—
held up by shed wings—my voice—this possibility.
You played basketball against St. John's,
when even six feet was tall—
I bowled against St. John's,
and now six feet is everything—
and we both hoisted balls,
and reached for some earthen sky—
yours to be in Tennessee,
me in my office, you in my memory—
and how good it is that the lion takes the buck—
and still the sun arcs across the horizons of our lives
and connects us through that other ring.

Susan saw a rainbow out the bathroom window,
and it was all to lower my head.

Part 2

Blessed holy
blessed holy
blessed father
blessed memories—

dropping popsicle sticks down
a King's Highway sewer grate in Brooklyn—
I was barely two,
going to the zoo in Rock Creek Park—
we drove through the creek
that flowed across the road
and didn't take the trolley home,
getting Sniffy-the-dog—

you drove a black and white taxi,
buying our first car—
a forty-nine powder blue Pontiac sedan—
our next was a '52 Willy's—
no one had ever seen fins before,
hitting a home run in the parking lot
of our garden apartment in Anacostia—
I couldn't understand how you could hit it so far,
teaching me to throw a curve ball
behind May's Department store, Levitown,
Long Island—fingers crosswise to the seams—
you made my palm burn when I caught you,
making a ten-pin at the Sunrise Lanes—
cross alley—you were robbed of a turkey
and a two-hundred game,
grinding a six-inch reflecting lens for my telescope
in the basement of our split level in Bellmore—
I knew the top forty by heart—
Murray-the-K and his Swinging Soiree,
submarine races,
going through puberty,

Tell me father, when did you first break?
Was it the marriage or the kids or the cancer
or the depression or the multiple sclerosis?
Was it the job, Dad? Was it the slow steady
decline? Was it the blood vessels breaking
one arteriole at a time?
Did you sell your soul to be a family man?
Did you ever cheat on Mom?
And when at last you were disabled
and fell back into disuse,
was it really a failure of nerve?

I learned about loving from you,
but you didn't know how to see it through,
and you didn't know how to fight.
I also needed to know how to fight, Father.
You only knew how to love and retire.

Father father, blessed father,
your shits smelled like you were king-of-the-john,
and I thought you were deep as you retreated
behind locked doors and open books.
Was there no peace?
No one ever knew what you wanted
until you were ready to die.
Joshua and Susan went back to the store three times
to get that Sony dual-deck stereo boom box
with recording option, and you said,
"I never had a present."
Who would have guessed?

Look, Dad, we loved each other,
but there was never much passion in it.
I had to get that from Mom.
She's doing all right.
I cut out a picture of you last Tuesday
and carried it around in my pocket.
It felt good to have you there.

Psalm

My father who art in Tennessee heaven,
hallowed in name
hallowed in memory
hallowed in cloth
peeping out behind shrouds,
your strong arms still hoist me to the sky

where I peer wide eyed,
"Look, Dad, Coney Island."

Holy blessed father yes
though I walk through the valley
of the shadow of your death,
your smiling face comforts me.

Yis-ga-dal vi-yis-kad-dash sh-may ra-baw.

Blessed father, sacred father,
you gave your life, your paychecks
your ravaged kidneys, your scarred retinas,
your heart. You gave us your heart.

Blessed are you in the house in North Bellmore
tho you couldn't make the stairs anymore,
blessed in Tennessee,
blessed in the ground,
blessed in your diabetic multi-system failure,
blessed in University Hospital,
blessed in the vein graft that replaced your femoral artery,
blessed in the surgery scar they cut from your groin to your foot,
blessed on dialysis,
blessed at your blessed microwave
        in which you heated the blessed liquid
        then ran it through the blessed tube
        in your blessed abdomen,
blessed in your amputated right big toe,
blessed in the suit against the podiatrist that cut you.

Yis-bor-ach, v'yis-ta-bach, v'yis-po-ar,
v'yis-ra-man, vi-yis-na-seh,
v'yis-ha-dor, v'yis-hal-leh, v'yis-ha-lal,
sh'ma d'ku-dah-sho, b'rich hu.

Blessed are you my father,
v'yim-a-roo, A-a-men.

Part 3

Oh, father, what have I left out—
the inertial guidance system you designed
    for the Atlas missile?
your thick cock?
the workbench you built in the basement?
the desk in Nancy's room?
the string sculptures you fancied and made
    until everyone you knew had one?
the smell of you crawling from your armpits
      hunched over the workbench
      sweat dripping from your chin
      your hairline receding
      your belly hanging over your belt?
the hairs growing out of your nose?

You taught me to shave,
to comb my hair by dousing it with water—
    part it on the left—
to tie my tie, my shoe laces, my tongue.
You took me to the deli, and we watched
    the surgeon slice lox,
then you let me order the bagels and rolls.

What have I forgot?
Your forehead, furrowed and deep?
your ugly clothes?
What were you thinking?
What am I?
Your eyes.

Your eyes saw the Brooklyn streets
    with horse drawn wagons.

Adored by your sisters,
    you were Uncle Yacey in Yiddish.
When I saw Aunt Laura's eyes last month
    at the wedding,
you were there too, watching.
Your spirit.
Praise to your spirit, Father,
    and to you who watched
and tried to never let us fall too hard.

Part 4

Praise to the yapping yelping call of the dogs.
Yapping yelping yawps praise the call of the dogs,
"call call," whistling wind,
"call call," calling, "come."

Yellow dogs and black birds speak.
The children are asleep,
but they stir to the sounds of sirens
and the neighborhood dogs.
We do not live on these rooftops any longer.
Clotheslines no longer stretch between neighbors.
Only the black birds and the yellow dogs make sense—
this yawp this call this paradise:
Caw caw caw caw
caw caw caw
and another car makes its way up
    North Jerusalem Road,
headlights casting shadows on the walls
    of my darkened room,
then up and away as the pitch of its swish passes

then lowers then fades:
Shhhhhhhhhhhhh,
Shhhhhhhhhh,
Shhhhhhhh

Robert Carroll

Road Trip

Michael F. Hoyt

When I finished graduate school in 1976, my father flew East so that we could meet and drive back to California together. We planned to hook-up in Chicago and head West, taking our time, a father-and-son road trip. I filled my little Japanese-import station wagon with my few belongings—a Persian rug, a bent-wood rocker, a couple of boxes of books, and a certificate declaring me a newly minted Ph.D.—said goodbye to New Haven, Connecticut (where I had gone to school), and drove to the Windy City, where he was spending a few days visiting old friends and family. After a night at my aunt and uncle's, Dad and I headed out for our big adventure.

Route 80 took us across Iowa and Nebraska, then south to Denver. A long conversation ensued as we motored along a concrete and asphalt ribbon of changing landscape, roadside motels, steak houses and truckers' breakfast spots. Small talk, jokes, family histories and mysteries, silences, discussions about school and my future, updates on family news, some sightseeing. Passing the Rockies, we entered Utah and decided to press on to Las Vegas.

Somewhere in southern Utah, somewhere along the way, somewhere in the night, a sign said, "Construction Ahead" and the road diverted. We turned off and took the side road, and then another. It was late and dark, and a sign directed us toward another detour. We were moving slowly on a dry scrabble dirt road. We passed fires in open oil drums and abandoned heavy equipment that looked like eerie dinosaurs in the shadows cast by our headlights. We slowly drove on for what seemed a long time, maybe another 45 minutes or an hour, following the road farther into the dark. It grew increasingly desolate and foreboding. We went further. There were no other cars, no more construction equipment. There had been no other signs, but we wondered if we had missed a turn. Just as we were discussing whether to turn around, it happened: The engine suddenly died!

"Oh shit!"

"Why'd you stop?" Dad asked.

"I didn't—the motor just stopped."

There was gas on the gauge. Turning the key did nothing. We tried, over and over.

"Don't flood it." We sat, then tried again. Nothing. We got out and opened the hood. Nothing. We wiggled a few wires. Nothing.

"We're fucked!" I muttered.

"No. We're stuck."

"What do we do?"

"We wait." said Dad.

"For what?"

"Help."

"From who?"

"We'll have to see."

"What if no one comes?"

"We'll see."

A long time passed. Suddenly, a large truck, an 18-wheeler, came around the curve. We stood by our car, in his headlights waving as he approached…the truck slowed but just kept going.

"Shit!" I cursed. Dad shook his head, saying nothing.

More time went by, maybe another hour. I turned the key again—still nothing. It was very dark and getting colder. Suddenly, another set of headlights! This time a car. We waved, but it barreled by, going too fast, not even slowing. The driver honked his horn as he disappeared into the night.

Eleven o'clock came and went. We sat in the car, hood up. Not talking much. Maybe an hour passed. Then another. It got even colder.

Then, headlights coming up the road toward us! We got out and waved. The pick-up truck slowed, then stopped. The driver rolled his window down.

"What's wrong?"

Dad spoke: *"We're stuck. The engine stopped and won't start. We've got plenty of gas."*

"Want me to take a look?"

"We'd sure appreciate it."

The man was white, wearing a jacket and a John Deere cap, looked to be in his mid or late 30's. His wife, bundled up, was sitting next to him. She was holding an infant or small child. Sleeping bundled up between them was a little girl, maybe 4 or 5, maybe a bit older.

He backed up his truck, faced his headlights under our hood, then got out and closed the cab door behind him. He leaned over the car and poked around, asking questions, wiggling this, checking that.

"What do you think?" Dad asked.

"I don't know—all your connections look OK."

"What do we do now?" I asked impatiently. Dad slipped me a look.

"It could be your gas line, but it sounds more electrical. Mind if I check a little more?"

The man went back to his pickup, behind the cab, and returned with a flashlight and a toolbox.

"Are you a mechanic?"

"Not really, but I like to fool around a little."

"Let me hold your light for you." said Dad.

Spark plugs were unscrewed and reversed. Nothing. Connections were loosened and retightened. Nothing. Hypotheses were formulated and tested. Nothing. Finally, he announced,

"Here it is! It's your rotor. It broke off. Too bad—I was hoping it was something we could rig up, at least to get you to town. There's nothing we can do—you'll need a new one. They should have one, but if not, they'll have to order it. You're going to need a tow into town."

"How far is it?" I asked.

"Not too bad—maybe an hour, little more."

I knew to be quiet. I let Dad speak.

"What should we do?"

"Well, your vehicle can't move, so I'll have to drive back and let them know you need help. It'll be better if I have them follow me to show them where you are."

"That's taking you way out of your way—I really appreciate all of your help."

"No problem."

The man went back to his truck, got in and talked with his wife for a few minutes. She listened, then nodded. He pulled up next to us.

"It'll take us maybe an hour to get there. There's an all-night service station. At this hour we should be able to get someone to come right away, so unless there's some problem, we'll be back in a couple of hours."

He turned around and drove off.

A couple of hours later, two sets of headlights appeared. The pickup pulled up next to us, followed by the tow truck. The driver got out.

"That wasn't too bad. I've told Joe what the problem is, and he'll tow you right to the gas station. The parts store is right next to it, and it opens up at 8 a.m. They should be able to get you back on the road. There's an all-night coffee shop you can wait in until it opens at 8."

"Thank you."

"*There's nothing more I can do. Like I said, you need a new rotor. You'll be OK with Joe. I think we're going to take off. We've got a way to go until we get home to Sacramento. But first, my wife's got some family in Los Angeles we're heading to see.*"

"*You've really helped us out.*" Dad reached into his pocket. "*I'd like to pay you for all of your time.*"

"*Don't worry about it.*"

"*That's very kind. But you really saved us, and it took you a long way out of your way in the middle of the night.*"

"*I was glad to be able to help.*"

"*I'd feel better if I could pay you—at least for your gas.*"

"*Nahh.*"

"*Well, then would you at least let me buy a little present for your girls?*" Dad had a couple of $20s in his hand.

"*It's not necessary.*"

"*No, but you've really been great.*"

The man paused. "*I don't want any money, but I'll tell you what you can do.*" We listened intently. "*Sometime, if you ever see someone who's stuck or needs a hand, help them out, OK?*"

Dad nodded. "*I understand. You're a good man.*" I listened.

He shook our hands, wished us well, and drove off as we called out, "*Thanks, again!*"

The tow driver hitched us up for the long ride into town.

"*Wow! What luck! He wouldn't even take any money. That was far out!*" I exclaimed.

"*Nice guy, huh?*" replied Dad.

"*You know, we never even found out his name.*"

"*Let's call him Sam, for short. Know what I mean?*"

I did. I bought some battery cables. Paid for them myself. You never know when someone might need a jump.

End Line

I've always been
a yin/yang front/back clear/blur
up/down life/death kind of guy
my own peculiar duality being
philosopher slash hypochondriac
win win characteristics
when you've been diagnosed
with advanced prostate cancer

finally the hypochondriac
has more than windmills to tilt with
the philosopher arming himself
with exactly the proper petard
an explosive statement
found in an email message
beneath the signature
of a cancer survivor's name
a perfect end line wily and wise
quote: I ask God:
"How much time do I have before I die?"
"Enough to make a difference."
God replies

"POOR DEVIL!"

in my early twenties
I went along with Dylan Thomas
boasting that I wanted to go out

not gently but raging
shaking my fist
staring death down

however this daring statement
was somewhat revised
when in my forties I realized
that death does the staring
I do the down
so I began hoping
it would happen to me
like it happened to the sentry
in all those
John Wayne Fort Apache movies
found dead in the morning
face down an arrow in the back
"Poor devil."
the Sergeant always said
"Never knew what hit him."

at the time I liked that…
the end taking me
completely by surprise
the bravado left in the hands
of a hard drinking Welshman
still wet behind the ears

older and wiser now
over seventy
and with a terminal disease
the only thing right about
what the Sergeant said
was the "Poor devil" part

"Poor devil"
never used an opening
to tell loved ones he loved them
never seized the opportunity
to give praise for the sun rise
or drink in a sunset
moment after moment
passing him by
while he marched through his life
staring straight ahead
believing in tomorrow
"Poor devil!"

how much fuller
richer and pleasing life becomes
when you are lucky enough
to see the arrow coming

Ric Masten
(Dedicated to Jim Fulks)

Burying the Past

Kristin Frykman

The day I saw the Santa Barbara premier of "The Way We Were," I knew I was stuck. The opening scenes of college life triggered a tsunami of tears and emotion. I was swamped with feelings of regret, anger, and frustration that lasted for weeks after the closing credits rolled.

Unconfronted for years, a bad decision was coming back to haunt me. I had recently moved to Santa Barbara with my husband and our plan had been that he, advanced degree now in hand, would pursue his new career while I returned to school to reach for mine. However, with jobs in multi-media production paying about half of what we expected, it was clear I would have to work full time in order for us to survive. I was mad.

My short piece of college life right after high school in Sweden was amazing and transformative. But it was not what I had been craving and was now desperate for: real academia.

I had made the choice of survival, taking the best job I could find to pay the rent and putting off full time college until some other time. "How could I have been so stupid?" was all I could think. I was mad. I was caught up in feeling let down, un-mentored, cheated out of what might have given my life direction and focus. I was mad—and, worse yet, knew my anger was pointless. But I couldn't shake it. No amount of internal dialogue would clear my head of this destructive fog.

Then I realized with whom I was really angry: it was me as a nineteen-year-old. Stupid girl. Suddenly I knew what to do. I rooted around in a box of old things and found a picture of me taken at the time I returned to California from Sweden. Sitting in a chair in the living room of my boyfriend's parents' home I am smiling but looking terrified. I had a wave of compassion and forgiveness for this girl. I looked into her eyes and said, "I forgive you. You did the best that you could in a scary situation."

I am grown up now and have to make choices based on where I am now, not where I should be. Then I did something without any premeditation or knowl-

70

edge of why I was doing it: I took that picture, kissed it, placed it in a plain white envelope, and buried it in the backyard. As I covered it with dirt I remember thinking the girl who made that decision is in the past—I am here in the present. That did it. It was like magic. The fog lifted, the clouds parted, and my anger retreated.

From that day on I keep a box on my closet shelf, covered with pretty paper bearing a label that reads, "THE PAST." From time to time I open it and put things inside. Sometimes I add tangible objects like photographs or a stone or a seashell, other times I only add the thought of something, a symbol, a lost vision.

But here is the important part: I never look inside.

Building on Progress

✦

(or as AA says: "Progress not Perfection")

Tapani Ahola

Positive Coaching

At the age of nine, my son began to play soccer. The team he played on had no coach and I was asked to sign up for the job. Although I had no previous experience in soccer, I did not want to refuse for the sake of my son.

Standing at the side of the soccer field for the very first time, I didn't know what to do. I observed the more experienced coaches who shouted to the boys things such as, "Watch the sides!" "Stay on-side!" and "Pass, pass, pass, don't sit on the ball!"

Before long, I was shouting just like the other coaches about the things that the boys were supposed to do and criticizing them for things they weren't supposed to do. It didn't take long for me realize that all my shouting was not having much effect. No matter how much or how loud I yelled, the boys would not pass the ball to one another as a soccer team should. Eventually, trying to avoid feeling like a fool, I decided to change tack. Instead of criticizing the boys, I decided to try and encourage them.

In the next game, the boys played much as usual. I kept quiet throughout the first half but at half-time I said, "Boys, I'm proud of you. I noticed that many times during the game you were going to pass the ball!"

The boys eagerly agreed. One of them said that he had been about to pass several times but that each time, someone else had been in the way.

During the second half, the boys passed the ball to one another significantly more often; when the game was over I acknowledged this development. I also said to them, "You're fortunate to play on a losing team. Losing is an excellent way to learn soccer and many very good players have started off playing on a losing team. Also, losing teams tend to have a good team spirit, right?"

The boys grew fond of playing on the team while I grew fond of soccer and them. I am now a soccer enthusiast and most weekends I'm off playing with my now winning team.

Originally in "Solution Talk," Ben Furman and Tapani Ahola, W.W. Norton & Co, Inc., 1992, NY and London. Reprinted with permission.

Yesterday, Today, and Tomorrow

Yesterday I went to Neil's house.
He was feeling better.
They discontinued the chemo
because of the vomiting.
It wasn't working anyway.
He said, "I can see my time is limited.
Before this I hoped for a miracle.
Now I just want to live for the time I've got.
My son's having it rough.
Yesterday he came and laid next to me in bed.
He told me it was important to just lie together."

"Yes," I said, "it's difficult for everyone,
and one thing you'll have to consider is when to stop
trying to live as long as possible and to begin
living as well as you can while you're dying.
How we die is as important a part of life as any we live—
What is said, what is done, what is left undone."

He shook his head, yes. The kettle on the stove began to whistle.
He fixed me a cup of tea. We sat on the couch together combing life through.
I read him the poem I wrote about his yellow skin, and he smiled.
"How am I doing?" he asked.
"How am I doing with this dying?"
and I knew that he knew that he was doing O.K.,
but I also knew he wanted to hear it from me, so I told him so,
and he smiled again and told me how important it was that I came,
and I knew it was true because it was what there was for me to do,
and I knew I would want the same, and as I left and drove south on Lincoln,
top down on my convertible, the Los Angeles sun shining, I had errands to do

and more people to see, and I felt honored and grateful, but weakened in my knees,
because I knew soon enough that he would be me.

Today I'm flying to Tennessee.
My son Josh and I are going to visit my family—
My mother, both sisters, their husbands and my nephews.
We'll spend the weekend on the lake and play in the water,
drink alcohol, and eat more than we ought to.

I want to go to the cemetery and remember the red mud
that covered the ground when they dug my father's grave.
I want to place a rock on his headstone,
lay myself down on the grass beside him,
feel the love and the longing for what was and what is not.
I want to put my arm around my mother and comfort her,
reminisce with my son about how Grandpop always knew the price of gasoline
and how he'd have been shocked that prices climbed to over two dollars a gallon
in Los Angeles, and how he'd smile when I told him it came back down to a buck fifty,
and how he'd remind me it's still less in Tennessee. I want to shoot squirt guns
with my nephews and throw stones in the lake, pick vegetables in my mother's
garden and take a walk in the woods. I want to go to my sister's office and say
hello to her staff,
drive my brother-in-law's Porsche, top down, shift into fifth. I want to see
Nancy's long-toothed smile and Daniel's sly grin and see Matey dance, and catch
up on all
that we've been through, and then on Monday, I will want to go home,
and when we arrive, be grateful to see my wife.

Robert Carroll

Learning What I Already Know

Erik John Frykman

The Summer of 1991 was the hardest period of my life. More than likely, I was what most would consider clinically depressed. I don't think it was just one single thing that led to this condition, but a string of events that all kind of gathered or piled onto one another.

Where to begin? From what I can remember, it all began with how I felt about the current state of my life. I was 25, about to turn 26, and had no idea what the hell I wanted to do with my life! I was in a horrible living situation that for almost three years had involved living in a tiny little studio apartment, right off of an incredibly busy thoroughfare, in a pretty odd/bad neighborhood. My relationship with my girlfriend had run its course, but because I cared about her so much, I didn't know what to do. I had ambitions of being a rock star and was working very hard at trying to do just that. And just as things were finally starting to happen for me and my band, one of the members (in a drug-induced rage) decided to give up music and said that he had had enough! Nice timing, considering we actually had a couple of record companies showing interest in us, but with the news of our instability said, "Thanks, but no thanks!" What could have been.

Another major event that contributed to my state was that in April of that year, my Dad and his wife decided to leave the parish they had been with for the past 13 or so years. Not that I blame them for what they had to do, it was obviously the right choice. It just came at a time when it seemed that all the things that I had come to know as normal in my life were falling apart. But it did help me learn that I tended to get comfortable with routine and more often than not, it would lead to complacency on my part.

But it wasn't just these situations that led to my demise. It just seemed that everywhere around me, every morning that I picked up the paper, every time I turned on the television, I was being reminded of what a horrible place this planet could be. The outrageous situation with Operation Desert Storm was a daily reminder of how insane thinking was beginning to run our lives. Not only on the part of Hussein, but on the part of our government that had basically created this Frankenstein. I became wrapped up in obsessing about everything that was out of my control. Driving myself crazy over things like how much I didn't know about life, when I should have been focusing on how much I did know! Stressing over people and situations that I had absolutely no control over. I had become an insomniac, sleeping maybe two to three hours a night (and that was on a good night!). I began to eat poorly and eventually started shutting out the people who mattered the most to me.

Finally, around September of that year, it felt like the sun had finally begun to start rising again on my life. At first, I wasn't sure why, but it didn't matter! I didn't feel miserable anymore! But why? What led to such a dramatic turnaround? Was it something that someone had told me? Done for me? Was there some magical sign that pointed me in the right direction? Some higher power at work? No...

Through that whole relentless period, the place that I finally found solace was...in myself. I can't exactly put my finger on it or define just exactly how it happened. But all I know is that once I got myself to the point of realizing that I didn't have to be the perfect human, didn't have to know everything there is to know, didn't have to have all the answers, I became a much happier person. As hard as it was, I ended the relationship I was in, moved into a one-bedroom apartment in a much better neighborhood, and decided to reevaluate how fortunate I was. And I finally started not only paying attention to, but clinging to, what so many people had been telling me all along. I was one of the luckiest people they knew because I actually got to do what I love for a living: make music and sell instruments. Wow...Life could have been a lot worse.

Simply put, I had to learn for myself, and no one else could show me that as long as I can get up in the morning, look at myself in the mirror, like what I see, and know that I am doing the best possible job to be the best possible person that I know how to be, that I must be doing okay! As long as I've done everything I can, to make my situation better without hurting anyone in the process, then that's all that I can ask of myself. No more, no less.

I know it may sound trite or cliche', but a quote from a recent Sheryl Crowe song kind of sums it all up for me:

"It's not having what you want, it's wanting what you've got..."

Survival Stories

Zoy Kazan

I have spent the past few months thinking about calamities, what constitutes them and how we survive them. I thought about my own life and those of the people who consult me and the process of story telling. It is my belief that in telling our stories we are able to move away from being the victims of calamities and move towards being authors of our lives. I recalled three stories of people who survived tragic events—stories that have impacted my own life:

The first story I remembered was told to me when I was an undergraduate studying history at Adelaide University. My history professor was a Holocaust survivor and talked in graphic detail about the years that he spent in the camp. My most graphic memory of his lecture was the description of many people sleeping together on a wooden pallet, skeletal with hunger, unable to turn over unless everyone else turned at the same time. He also described the brutal conditions of enforced work in a stone quarry, where many of his friends died from starvation and exhaustion. It is too late for me to ask my professor how he survived this ordeal. But I did have a sense, in listening to him speak, that his awareness of the suffering of those around him and his compassion for their plight may have had something to do with it. I will remember this man's story for the rest of my life and I think that part of the reason that it stays with me with such clarity is that his rage at the suffering of his community was still palpable and was offered as a gift to generate awareness and compassion in his undergraduate audience. In telling the story year after year, my professor remembered the dead and honored them. It is probably the most meaningful gift I could have received and remains as a legacy to stir me out of my complacency to this day.

Another story that comes to mind is that of Janet Frame, who wrote an autobiographical trilogy about her life that became the subject of the film, "Angel at my Table." Frame was misdiagnosed with schizophrenia and spent eight years of her life in mental institutions in New Zealand in the 1950s. During this time she was subjected to over two hundred applications of ECT, each one being "the equivalent, in degree of fear, to an execution." She was scheduled for a leucotomy, a disaster that was narrowly averted when the superintendent of the hospital read a newspaper article announcing that she had been awarded the Hubert Church award for her collection of short stories entitled, "The Lagoon." Frame wrote about her survival in Seacliff Hospital thus:

"In the back ward I became part of a memorable family that I have described individually in Faces in the Water. It was their sadness and courage and my desire to 'speak' for them that enabled me to survive..."[1]

There seems to be a common thread between Frame and my professor: both of them survived terrible tragedies and were able to focus on the plights of others who did not survive. In telling their stories, they honored the victims, but also were able to move forward in their own lives. Both people witnessed terrible oppression, but in caring for their friends they did not have time for self-pity. Instead, they were able to name the injustices and leave a legacy that would help ensure that they would not be repeated.

The third story is that of my father, who survived being a prisoner of war on Crete during WWII. After escaping from the POW camp, he and his unit of men were sheltered in villages and hidden in caves until they could escape by boat and were finally picked up by an allied submarine near the coast of Italy. My father suffered serious injuries from a land mine explosion on mainland Greece and a subsequent plane crash on Mount Hagen in New Guinea. In 1947, he endured a primitive spinal laminectomy that saved him from becoming a paraplegic. As a child, I never knew that my father had a disability and never thought of him as injured in any way. It was only as an adult that I became aware of my father's struggle with sciatic nerve pain. In the last 15 years of his life, the pain became worse and he underwent several surgeries to insert a TENS device alongside his damaged spine. It was necessary for him to be conscious during this process so that he could give feedback to the surgeon that the device was in the correct position for blocking the pain. During these operations, the surgeon, who was also a war historian, invited him to talk about his war experiences. Because he had a thorough knowledge of the campaigns in the Middle East and in the Pacific, he could ask questions of my father in a detailed way and invited him to tell the story in all of its complexity. Later on, my father described this doctor as "the only one who ever really listened to me." I noticed the healing effect of this storytelling on my father. He became more mellow and loving, and the impatience and irascibility that had been a feature of his personality evaporated. In being a

---

1.   Quotes from "Angel at my Table": Frame, J. (1984). *Angel at my table*. New York: George Brazillier.

witness and co-author of the story, the surgeon helped my father debrief from the tragedies of fifty years ago and helped to free him of the pain and the burden that he had been carrying.

As I wrote this piece, the tragic events of 9/11/01 were unfolding in New York and Washington. As the week has passed and the death toll has risen, there have been news reports of posters, photographs, descriptions, and names of the dead and missing on storefronts, scaffolding, and buildings. There have been stories of great heroism: the man who stayed with his wheelchair-bound friend on the 22nd floor; the guide dog who managed to lead his owner down all those flights of stairs and keep going for two blocks until the towers collapsed; the firefighters, police and ambulance drivers who lost their lives trying to get people out of the building. It is the stories that have most impacted me more than the endless pictures of the tragic scene. The stories have helped me grieve and helped me really appreciate the heroism and the compassion of those involved. As the tragedy recedes for those of us who did not lose friends or loved ones, I think it is important for us all to bear witness to the stories of those who did. It is the telling and re-telling of these stories that helps us to re-member the dead. And in the re-membering process we incorporate the meaning of their lives into our own.

Bilateral Orchectomy

never could
look up words in the dictionary
in a high school assignment
writing an autobiography
I described my self as a unique person
scribbled in the margin
the teacher's correction fairly chortled
"unique" not "eunuch"
how could he have known
that one day I would actually become
a misspelling

backed against the wall
by advanced prostate cancer
I chose the operation
over the enormous ongoing
expense of chemical castration
"No big deal," I thought at the time
what's the difference
they both add up to the same thing

but in the movies these days
during the hot gratuitous sex scene
I yawn…bored…
wishing they'd quit dicking around
and get on with the plot
and on TV the buxom cuties

that titillate around the products
certainly aren't selling me anything

I realize now that
although it would probably kill them
the guys who went chemical
still have an option
I don't

philosophically I'm the same person
but biologically
I'm like the picture puzzle
our family traditionally puts together
over the holidays
the French impressionist rendition
of a flower shop interior
in all it's bright colorful confusion

this season I didn't work the puzzle
quite as enthusiastically…
and for good reason
this year I know pieces are missing
where the orchids used to be

"So?" says I to myself
"You're still here to smell the roses!"

Ric Masten

Nigel Learns to Make His Nightmares into Goodmares

Ben Furman

It was a Friday morning when Nigel and his parents where having breakfast together. Nigel was drinking chocolate and eating cereal. His parents where drinking coffee and eating sandwiches. *Listen, Nigel*, said father. *We will go out to dinner with our friends this evening and you will go to granny for the night.*

Nigel felt like crying but he did not say a word. Tears were running down his cheeks right into his cereal bowl. *Oh my*, said mother, *you are crying. What are you crying for? You like granny. Don't you like to sleep over at her place?*

Nigel could not help it. He started to cry out loud. Father started to get nervous. *What has got into him?* Father asked the mother. *Don't get nervous, you. It may have something to do with his nightmares.*

I see, said father.

During the past few weeks Nigel had had nightmares almost every night. The nightmare was always the same. Big lorries were chasing him trying to run over him. The nightmare used to wake him up in the middle of the night. After that he would sit on his bed and just cry and cry. Mother and father had to calm him down and it could take up to fifteen minutes before he fell asleep again.

Evenings Nigel was afraid to go to sleep. One evening when mother had already given him a good night kiss and told him good night, he said, *I am not going to sleep at all. I will stay awake all night. That way I won't have that awful nightmare.*

C'mon, don't say that. You must sleep at night. Everyone must sleep at night. If a person does not sleep at night, he is so tired next day that he cannot do anything.

I don't care, said Nigel. *Anyway, I will stay awake all night*, said Nigel decisively.

In fact, Nigel did fall asleep in no time but if it only would have been possible, there is no doubt about it, he would have stayed up all night in order to escape his nightmares.

Nightmares or not, you will go to granny anyway. We have not had a chance to go out, just me and your mother, and parents need some time on their own too, said father impatiently.

Yes, but we can inform granny about the nightmares. Granny can, for example, leave the door open to Nigel's room. When the door is open, granny will hear if Nigel wakes up and can come and soothe him.

When the parents left Nigel to granny's for the night that evening they were so busy that they simply forgot to inform granny about Nigel's nightmares. Nigel thought to himself that he will do it himself when granny puts him to bed.

When granny was reading the bedtime story to Nigel, he said, *You know granny, I have a nightmare almost every night. It is always the same awful dream. There are huge trucks trying to run me over. I cry in my dream and then I wake up. Mom or dad comes to comfort me and it may take quite some time before I fall asleep again.*

Granny listened to Nigel attentively and then whispered into his ear.

Listen, Nigel, I can tell you a secret about nightmares. Do you want to hear it? she said. Nigel was puzzled. He nodded to signal that he wanted to know what the secret was.

There are no nightmares, said granny. Nigel did not understand a thing.

Granny explained: *Look, the fact is that all dreams have a happy ending. Only sometimes a person may wake up in the middle of a dream, at a moment when something exciting is happening so that he misses the end of the dream. I can bet that your dream with those trucks has a happy ending, but you have to continue to see it in order to see what happens.*

Nigel wondered, *could it really be so.*

Do you remember the Bambi video? asked granny all of a sudden. Nigel nodded.

Do you remember that there is an exciting moment when Bambi's mother dies? That part is so tragic that even I, an older person, always cry when I see it. Don't you think it would be horrible if at that moment there was an electricity blackout and you could not see the film any further? The film has a happy ending but only if you have a chance to see it to the end.

But I don't know how the dream ends because I always wake up when the trucks start chasing me.

So you do but perhaps you would not wake up if you knew how the dream continues.

How does it continue then? asked Nigel in bewilderment.

You can never know for sure but you can always imagine the happy ending. What do you suppose will happen after the trucks have been chasing you?

I don't know said Nigel. He was thinking.

I don't know either but I can imagine that you would find that the trucks would not run over you but they would only come close to you and perhaps they would want to give you something. What might they want to give you?

Nigel got excited about the thought. He said, *"An ice hockey racket!"*

An ice hockey racket, repeated granny. *I should have guessed that, knowing that you are such a champion ice hockey player. So the dream might continue with the trucks surrounding you, you would lower your head and you would start to cry. When you would lift up your head again, to your surprise the truck drivers would have come out of the trucks and they would ask you to come inside the trucks. Inside each of them there would be a kind of a sport shop and you would be asked to choose one item from each one of them. Would you like that? If something like that would happen, would that make the nightmare become a good dream?*

Sure, said Nigel.

I am not saying that the dream will continue like that. You can come up with something else instead. But now that you go to sleep, think about how you want your dream to end. If you think hard of the happy ending, you will see that your nightmare will turn into a goodmare.

What is a goodmare, asked Nigel in bewilderment.

It is the good dream behind the nightmare that comes to us when we have the courage to see how the bad dreams end, explained granny.

When Nigel put his head to the pillow, he imagined how the trucks surrounded him and how he was invited inside of them. In one of them he chose an ice hockey racket that had the original signature of his favourite player.

From another truck he got a fantastic ice hockey helmet and from the third truck he got a cool shirt. When he was falling asleep he was almost hoping to have the very dream that he had so much been afraid of.

When mom and dad came to pick him up the next morning, they asked granny how the night had gone.

We were going to tell you last evening that Nigel has recently had a recurring nightmare but we were so much in a hurry that we forgot all about it. Did Nigel wake up in the night because of his nightmare?

No, he didn't. He slept throughout the night like a log.

That's surprising. I think that must be like the first night in two weeks when he did not have his nightmare. What magic has granny been using again? Asked mother smiling.

I just told Nigel how to turn nightmares into goodmares. Nothing magic about that.

By the way, Nigel, how did you manage? Did you see the end of the dream?
I tried but it didn't work. The dream just never came. Granny smiled and patted Nigel on the head.

Next evening when Nigel was already in bed browsing through a picture book, mom went to talk with him. *Listen Nigel, I have never told you, but sometimes I have nightmares too. Not every night but every now and then I have the same unpleasant nightmare. Could you please tell me what granny told you about how to turn nightmares into goodmares?*

Christmas Anxiety

The Patient Nose: A Biopsychosociospiritual Story

Israela Meyerstein

I looked intently in the mirror, scanning my face. Facial expression, after all, is the purveyor of personality, conveying who one is to the world. The eyes are windows to the soul; the nose has been called the seat of self-recognition (Hay, 1988). In Chinese medicine, the skin is thought of as a "third lung," engaging in processes of exchange, intake, and excretion with the environment (Connelly, 1994). These familiar features, which I had come to know, were now at risk of changing forever.

It had all started with growing fears about skin damage. I presented the symptoms to my Skin Doctor, who diagnosed a pre-cancerous condition and prescribed topical medication. During the course of treatment my nose erupted into a bleeding crater. A biopsy revealed an infiltrative basal cell the size of a dime, perhaps bigger. I was immediately referred to the Skin Cancer Surgeon and to a Plastic Surgeon, who would be needed to repair the substantial wound following surgery.

The Skin Cancer Surgeon was intelligent and precise, as was his microscopic technique that carefully mapped and excised the tumor. His quietly confident manner made me feel comfortable depending on his care. At first I found his surgical certainty reassuring. However, once surgery was over, he became inaccessible and nonresponsive to calls.

"To write prescriptions is easy, but to come to an understanding with people is hard."—Franz Kafka

The now nickel size gaping wound was transferred to the hands of the Plastic Surgeon to close. Surprised by its size, without forewarning me, he ordered general anesthesia so that he could more easily move portions of my forehead skin down to my nose. Upon awakening I had no idea what had been done, or what I looked like. The traumatic surgery completed, and the ugly stitches removed, I was left with a large scar transcending my nose…Scars represent life's wounds, I reflected. Some are visible some are not.

I looked around at people whose faces were intact, whose skin seemed to protect them from the environment. I felt different, alien, and damaged. The Surgeon even told me a story about a psychiatrist whose facial expression acquired a puzzled look after such surgery. As a result, his patients could no longer tell how he was reacting to their words, not a comforting thought for someone whose livelihood was based on talking face to face with people.

Recuperation provided little time to ponder the recent trauma. Within a month, I experienced other pinpoint bleeds on my temple and tip of my nose, and biopsies identified more cancer cells. Furthermore, a routine visit to the gynecologist revealed an ovarian cyst that must now be watched. What was happening here? My health fears intensified along with a systemic curiosity about my body as a larger system. Could these incidents be related to each other? Had coexistent processes led to toxins and negativity being caught in the skin instead of eliminated from my body? The Skin Cancer Surgeon insisted they were due only to sun exposure on a fair skinned complexion "because you are not African-American," he said. What about diet and nutrition? What about immune function? And what about emotions and spiritual disposition? He summarily responded to my thoughtful questions by pointing out the irrelevancy of all these factors and scheduled the next surgery.

I felt angry at being dismissed and disconfirmed. I felt helpless to stop the emergence of new cancer cells, but this time my spirit rebelled. I had enough of being a patient patient. Triggered by a terrible dream in which I watched a woman, already wounded, being chased by a man (whose name resembled the surgeon's) wielding a knife, I realized my spirit was telling me not to trust so full-heartedly.

"Healing proceeds from the depths to the heights"—Carl Jung

And so in the interregnum of fear, despair, and helplessness, I started to say "no" and make my own choices, thus beginning my healing journey. I spoke with my Skin Doctor, a woman who listened to my fear, confusion, and intuition. "Remember," said the Doctor. "It's your nose; all the doctors are excellent but it's still your nose." Concerned about my shuttling between different doctors and feeling alone and burdened, the Skin Doctor stepped forward to be the central coordinator of care.

"A doctor does more by the moral effect of his presence on the patient and family than anything else."—William James

Feeling heard and validated by my Skin Doctor's support, I began responding to my body's symptoms in a way that felt coherent with my beliefs and intuitions. I sought out a homeopath who did a general physical, listened to my story, then shared his views on treating cancer systemically. He supported all the biomedical efforts and outlined a four-pronged strategy that included dealing with the tumor, cleansing the body of toxins (physical and emotional), altering nutritional patterns to rebuild immune system functioning, and embarking on a behavioral, emotional, spiritual journey to break bonds of confining habits and strive for a change of heart.

Bolstered by a plan, I delayed the surgery, found a new Skin Cancer Surgeon and new Plastic Surgeon who listened respectfully to my views and needs and were willing to collaborate with me. I began a several-months project of physical and spiritual cleansing and repair.

"Each patient carries his own doctor inside him. They come to us not knowing that truth. We are at our best when we give the doctor who resides within each patient a chance to go to work."—Albert Schweitzer

I equipped myself with knowledge through reading and learning about others' struggles. I validated my own intuitive experience as a primary guide. I released emotions through acupuncture and exercise. I embraced positive affirmations, visualization, and prayer. Shedding fears and paralysis, I now wore the badge of courage, self-direction, and self-confidence.

Doing everything I could on my own behalf, I had become self-guided, while interdependently collaborating with helpers, I focused my attention on the attainment of joy through music and prayer. My chavurah or friendship group lent their caring prayer in a strengthening healing circle.

Finding that telling details of the upcoming surgery weighed me down with anxiety, I opted to put such conversations aside so I could maintain my lightened spirit. My Skin Doctor had agreed to redo a biopsy. Even after it was reported negative, the doctors still felt the surgery was warranted. Meanwhile, returning to monitor the progress of my cyst at the gynecologist, I was told, "Congratulations, its gone. Your body is healing itself." Amazed and encouraged, I delayed the upcoming surgery on my nose for another month. I intensified my efforts, concentrating in the last month on diet, nutrition, visualization, and prayer.

"The power of the imagination is a great factor in medicine...Ills of the body may be cured by physical remedies or by the power of the spirit acting through the soul."—Paracelsus

The day of the surgery arrived. I had braced myself for having my nose cut open again with more disfiguring surgery. Who knew what it would look like? The surgeon and residents visually confirmed the large tumor cell. True to his word, however (or perhaps to humor me), he did another biopsy. While waiting for the results, I drew a picture of my situation to manage my anxiety. I pictured myself lying on the table, faced by a doctor whom I trusted as an agent of healing, feeling G-d's presence shining through the surgical lamp. All around me, I visualized the caring glances of those who supported me.

My musings were interrupted by the nurse calling me back to the operating room for surgery. The surgeon greeted me with the words, "good news," and then he continued, "There's nothing there." I was in shock, overcome with emotions after the roller coaster ordeal. I broke down crying, filled with great relief and bliss. I hugged my husband and the surgeon for being respectful of my wishes and doing the unusual repeated biopsy before cutting.

I shared the happy news with family and supportive friends. When the excitement died down, it was replaced by reflection, humility, and deep gratitude, less for my intensive efforts and more for the serendipitous grace of G-d's healing. I had made myself as open to healing as I knew how, then turned the rest over to G-d. I had been patient with myself, with my nose. In fact, I had been a good obedient patient. Then I became a better, self-determining, knowing patient. I put trust in my gut instincts, took responsibility for decisions, and cultivated my spirit. I gave myself credit and permission to call the shots even in the face of knowledgeable, experienced doctors. They knew science and predictable rules, but they didn't often leave space for exceptions.

I wondered, where did the healing take place? Was it inside, in between, or beyond? Indeed, I though to myself, when all is said and done, really the patient nose.

References

Hay, L. (1988). *Heal your body: The mental causes for physical illness and the meta-physical way to overcome them.* Santa Monica, CA: Hay House.

Connelly, D. M. (1994). *Traditional acupuncture: The law of the five elements,* 2nd ed. Traditional Acupuncture Institute.

Quotes

Kafka: Glatzer, N. N. (Ed.) A Country Doctor. In *The collected stories.* New York: Schocken, 1971, p.223.

Jung: Barasch, M. I. *The healing path.* New York: Penguin Books, 1993, p.60.

William James: Myers, G. E. *William James: His life and thought.* New Haven: Yale University Press, 1986, p.373.

Schweitzer: McGarey, G. T. and Stearn, J. *The physician within You: Medicine for the millennium.* Deerfield Beach, Florida: Health Communications, 1997, p.23.

Paracelsus: Hartman, F. *Paracelsus: Life and prophecies.* Blauvelt, New York: Rudolf Steiner, 1973, p.11-12.

The Language of Letting Go

Usually the rain helps me drift off to sleep
But tonight I am lying wide awake.
I'm tired enough to dream but there's something deep inside me—
A feeling I cannot seem to shake.

Standing on the cusp of some fateful new beginning
Sure there's a future I can't know
The world keeps on turning
And I realize it's time to learn
The language of letting go.

I've battled it for years in a struggle never ending
To win just this cold and lonely night
Now I understand that I've only been pretending to keep things neat
And make it all seem right.
In hindsight I can see that appearance is deceiving
I even bought the lines in my own show
The world just keeps on turning
And I realize it's time to learn
The language of letting go.

It's time to let go of a past that never changes
No matter how I analyze the facts
Or rearrange it.
Time to let go of the things I can't control…
Time to shed these anchors on my soul.

It's getting nearly dawn, and the rain is falling harder
Like tears the angels freely shed
I'm crying with them too, and it feels like holy water falling down

And pooling in my bed.
The lessons I am learning I will have to learn again
If anything, my progress will be slow
But the world just keeps on turning
And I realize it's time to learn
The language of letting go.

It's time to say, I'm letting go....
Usually the rain helps me drift off to sleep....

Punishing in North Beach

Lars Frykman

Back in my college days, I had a friend named Luke. We'll call him Luke because that's what his name could have been. He was never innocent and never needed his name changed to protect the innocent.

I thought Luke was cool, very cool. No matter what you needed or what you wanted to do, Luke could "procure" it for you.

One night while waiting for a "procurement" to happen, Luke, his brother (who wasn't quite as hip as Luke but still pretty cool), and I were shooting pool at a local tavern that Luke liked because of the huge "Miller High Life" mirror they had over the bar. (I could go into why he liked that mirror so much, but that's a whole 'nother story.)

We were having a good time shootin' pool when this guy comes up to me and flicks my hair (which at the time was about shoulder length) and says, "Where'd you get that hair?"

"I grew it," wondering matter-of-factly where the hell this guy was going with his line of questioning.

Next he shoves me and says, "Where the hell'd you get those bars! You don't look like you deserve to wear them!"

I should explain this guy looked about seven feet tall, had a typical "high and tight" Marine haircut and had a tattoo that said, "I'll kill you" on his shoulder.

I also should explain that I was wearing my father's old Army field jacket that had his captain's bars on it. I thought it was terribly cool and never thought I would offend or dishonor anything or anybody by wearing it.

That jacket earned me the nickname, "Captain Largent, savior of the universe!"

That's a whole 'nother story too: the jacket and how I got that name.

Anyway, back to the Marine in the bar. After the challenge about my hair and Dad's bars, I looked around and saw that Luke and his brother had become aware of my predicament and were, uh, standing ready to speak with their pool queues in hand and looking at me like, "are we gonna dance or what?"

You have to understand that I was quite naive and quite the pacifist and if anybody's name needed changing in this story it was mine! I'm thinkin', "SHIT, this is going to turn into a scene from an old John Wayne movie if you don't think of something quick!"

So here's what I came up with. I said to the Marine, "Look, my Dad was a chaplain in the National Guard. He gave me these bars and I don't think he would have given them to me if he didn't think I deserved them!" Then I got ready to duck, but instead of putting his fist in my mouth the Marine said, "Wow, you're all right, guy. What are ya drinkin?"

The look of relief on my face must have been one for the ages. He proceeded to get me a Bass. Luke and his brother went back to their game and I did my best to be cool in North Beach.

Prague '97

I try to imagine what life was really like when Prague was in her glory
and
armor had a knight.
Castles, crowns and forests green, sweet damsels bowing to their
queen.
Her city streets meander, her buildings draped in art.
Gargoyles with their watchful stares look down on flowers
everywhere.
Now, nights are but a time of day, and spotlights take the dark away.
The muses still but music make, Bach and Mozart thrive.
Dvorak and Smetana in their wake.
Tourists are the subject, politics replaced the king.
Beauty is their mistress, art and music is their queen.
Economics is in the counting house.
Now that communism's dead
And Prague reclaims her glory for she has grown a whole new head.
If you listen closely you can hear their voices ring.
This is the beginning of Prague's perpetual spring.

Jeri Inger

Stuckness 101

Mary Curran

Over the past 30 plus years, I have walked the path of "stuckness" with individuals and organizations as a therapist, a facilitator and as an organizational consultant. Stuckness seems to be part of our human conditioning, particularly due to a tendency to form habits and assign anything possible to patterns that appear to succeed, at least for the moment. These behaviors and responses are quickly forgotten so that we can get on with more immediate and challenging encounters in our life. They are assigned to the archives of the unconscious, on reserve for any similar stimulus to arrive in the future and ready to evoke an automatic response.

An intriguing phenomenon that I have become more aware of through my Buddhist practice is the propensity of the mind to be forever active in interpreting reality. While we experience these messages from the mind as "the reality," on most occasions, the mind could have delivered an entirely different perspective and we would have considered it just as "real." Because a stimulus will produce an emotional response, as well as a need for understanding its meaning, self-awareness is a critical practice if we are to ever deliver ourselves from the many ways in which we can get caught in the mire of "stuck-tivity."

- Out of fear for a child's safety, a parent may continue to set the same restrictions on a teenager that were necessary when the child was in middle school, rather than encouraging a growing degree of self-responsibility in a developing young adult.

- Living together for several years can have a couple responding to one another from internal expectations rather than allowing new ideas, feelings, growth, and responses. Deep listening to another requires that we let go of old sets of beliefs and assumptions in order to hear, even those we know so well, in a new and fresh way.

- In a rapidly changing work environment, organizations are challenged with the need for continuous renewal and the ability to reassess the effectiveness of work processes. Since a certain amount of security resides in the comfort of doing things in a tried and true manner, managers are challenged to create collaborative environments that respect individuals as well as continually consider the need for change.

In order to maintain flexible psychic muscles so that we are prepared to keep a balance between innovation and tradition in our lives, I have found four practices that are very helpful.

Interview the mind. Investigate how it came to such a conclusion. Trace back the trigger event and try to identify what is an observable fact, an inference, where I have added meaning to an event, what feelings this event aroused, and how I may have "force fit" this interpretation of events into prior experience. For example, when my husband died, my relationship with my three step-children had to be reexamined, since he was no longer present to hold the family together. This was actually an opportunity to create the relationship we each wanted, but so easy to feel rejection, make assumptions and try to hold on to the way it has been. Many times over the past year I've had to ask myself, "But, how do I know that? What am I really feeling? Why am I assuming this to be true? Call. Ask. Find out!"

Propose alternate interpretations. Because we are so predisposed to accept as reality whatever the mind says is so, it helps to raise questions and possible doubts. Immediately propose other ways of interpreting what catches one's attention in order to help the mind recognize that it may have just made up some facts out of thin air. If we can consciously propose alternate interpretations, the mind is likely to be less certain of its position and head off the avalanche of emotions that generally follow such certainty. I have a friend who has been working with a mediator in an effort to get through a very difficult divorce for over a year. The mediator and almost everyone she knows has said that it is time to turn the divorce over to her lawyer. Recently a few of us spent a weekend retreat together and when she asked for our assistance and proposed talking just one more time to her husband, she was finally able to confidently agree to go to the lawyer instead after she had listened to alternate ways of interpreting what to her had been so much a part of lifelong patterns. The possibility that her husband is simply incapable of the level of cooperation that she is looking for seemed new to her. She was so accustomed to taking care of him that it had never occurred to her that he had just not developed the skills necessary to work successfully with a mediator.

Remain in the present. Because patterns are so tied to the past and hold some kind of desperate hope that they may do well by us forever, it is easy to lose awareness of the subtleties that make this situation different than anything that we have ever encountered before. By staying in the present, the mind does not become confused by historical perceptions (generally altered to fit new circumstances). It is free to give full attention to what is true reality in the moment and less likely to generate the fear that can so easily grab hold of us when we are attempting to foresee the future. The only time frame in which we can really be effective is the present. While planning for the future does have its place, it needs to be kept in balance with living fully in the present. We are less likely to get stuck in any pattern when we are taking in valuable information about our current reality.

Deliberately experiment. Try "outrageous" behaviors—outrageous only to me because the are outside my patterned response. Recently I have been determined to stay ahead of the arthritis that has been crippling my knees. A physical therapist observed that I have not been swinging my hips when I walk, forcing my feet to point out, which puts all the pressure on my knees. To change a pattern as old as walking takes concentration and a strange sense of disequilibrium. Now, I consciously think of shifting weight, which swings my hips, which point my feet where they belong and takes pressure off of my knees. Somehow as a teenager I decided that swinging hips were wanton and I probably could not have been convinced otherwise at the time.

In working with the Hospice support group, I have found that death of a loved one presents an opportunity to get unstuck from many parts of our life that may be limiting us in ways we had not considered. Since life after the loss of a parent, spouse, child, or close friend changes our life as we could not have imagined, it is important to not lose this opportunity to shake ourselves loose from the patterns that no longer serve us well. Many will try to avoid the pain of grief by staying busy, finding a substitute relationship or sinking into depression. I have found that there is never so important a time to remain fully conscious and track what the mind is saying about reality. When you really listen to what your mind is telling you, you become less likely to take it so seriously.

There are great advantages for exercising our psychic muscles in everyday events—those related to grief, happiness, the whole gamut of emotion—so that one is better prepared and possibly more open to the inevitably more difficult moments like the death of a loved one or even one's own death. It's a honing stone: patience and repeated practice hone the blade. It's the same idea that to play the piano well, one needs to practice almost everyday!

For Allison from her Mother

Nursing

Your body curled in my lap
Your warm mouth at my breast
Your fierce eyes grow thoughtful
and then glaze into sleep.

What is it like to be helpless, tiny, cradled safe in the body's heat
Melting into darkness?
I had forgotten
But now, almost, I remember.

I have become softness
My angled breasts down pillows
My belly rounded from your body's mold
On my lips, lullabies.

With milk given and taken
Is the cut birth cord rewoven in the bone
Irrevocable now down all the years, in love or silence.
In your cells my form
In my eyes your image
We grow, each marked by the other
The veining in the leaf, the mica in the rock.

October 1983

Cleaning my Daughter's Room As She Leaves For College

Surely this is the true archeology, the dig, the tell,
We the explorers with our maps and brushes,
Aerial photographs of memory,
Layers of life on the shelving, layers of dust.
Small dinosaurs roamed here once,
Now encased in plastic instead of amber.
Fossil trilobites,
Coins and painted dresses,
Clay pots, flutes,
Soft fur medicine bag,
A complex civilization.

How do we choose and sort—
What goes to the museum somehow building in the attic?
Your first, favorite doll asleep in the upstairs hallway,
Shawls, hats, handwritten stories,
The oddly shaped pieces of the game we made together
Kept whole now for future children to try, touch,
Say "what a strange thing, what was it for?"—

We turn to each other with full hands—
What do we give away, throw away,
All this energy of making,
All the love in these forgotten objects, how do we hold on to
Love, still living in an empty room,
In the clothes and vessels left behind
Which still hold voices, stories of our hearts.

June 2001
Ellen Berman

Getting Unstuck Through Pain

David Baum

My motto? No pain, no pain.

—Carol Leiffer (on the Comedy Channel)

What's often needed for either getting unstuck or helping others in the process is a firm and measured kick-in-the-ass. In my experience, the benefits to not changing are so deeply rooted in one's fear patterns that something totally anathema to the individual is often needed to break the unconscious benefits that keep one stuck. The benefits to not changing are oftentimes so strong that they provide an insurmountable force to action. Without these benefits, movement would be a graceful affair.

But somewhere, somehow a gain prevails that keeps the individual tied into a long-standing and painful cycle. Without addressing these benefits in a creative and forceful manner, their power is often hypnotic and stubborn.

What then can be done? How do you respond quickly to such a difficult situation? In the brilliant work of social psychologist Kurt Lewin and his model of Force Field Analysis (Hall & Lindzey, 1978), Lewin postulates that when we create additional benefits for change the human psyche generally responds by only adding more creative barriers. It's why New Year's Eve resolutions rarely hold. The intention to stop smoking, for instance, is met with a complex rationale of addiction and need. Every motivator we add ("If I stop smoking, I'll splurge on a weekend to New York.") is unconsciously rebuffed by another resistor ("I didn't really want to go to New York.") The more dedicated the intention, the more resolute the resistance strategy.

Thus, the only way to enable real movement is not through addition of benefit or "positive motivation" but through the mitigation of these unconscious blocks.

The Japanese martial art of art aikido offers a principle called "randori." It means to be in the right place, with the right technique, at the right time, with the right level of power.

Randori teaches us that the goal in working with personal change is to focus on the "negative" side of transition. We can do this by creating scenarios that are worse than the fear of breakthrough. We make not changing so highly undesirable that it outweighs the risk to change. Individuals need to feel that the current state of non-action is more painful than movement. The question becomes: how?

We've found a very effective strategy, somewhat controversial and unique, but very potent: We use a "penalty."

Case in point: I had a friend who for three years had been struggling to get the first chapter of his dissertation completed. No matter what he did, he was constantly finding excuses and reasons for delaying the task at hand. This put him in a desperate situation, because the more he delayed, the worse he felt about himself and then the more he would procrastinate. A typical vicious cycle.

One day I said to him, "Bob. Do you really want to get this done?"

"Yes," he emphatically implored.

"Terrific. How much is it worth to you to get your first chapter completed? Five hundred dollars? A thousand dollars? Five thousand dollars? Be real but aggressive."

"Oh, God. I'd pay five thousand to get it going."

"Fine," I said. "Write me a check for five thousand dollars and postdate it one month from today. If I don't have a first draft in my hand by that date, I will cash the check and send the money to the Republican National Committee (he was an ardent Democrat)."

My goal was to create something so painful he would rather have walked through burning coals than miss his deadline. He hemmed and hawed for a few minutes, but I kept repeating the question, "Are you really serious about this?" The more he protested his intentions for change, the more the idea seemed to be an obvious Bell-weather test. It was time to get off the pot.

The response? His fear of financial loss was over-powering. $5000 was a fortune to him at the time, representing a quarter of his life's savings. Add to this the money would go to the Republicans and the force was enough to break his fear patterns. Once broken through the use of a "penalty," his emotional energy propelled him forward. Bob became a man possessed. Finally free from the indulgence of his self-inflicted judgment his creative energies went to a more productive use. He had the first chapter completed in two weeks and a finished dissertation in four months!

Could he have canceled the check and not met his obligations? Of course. But then he would have had to deeply confront his lack of commitment to breakthrough. And we agreed that if he took this action he would never again be allowed to complain to anyone about his lack of completion (an almost non-stop topic of conversation). He finally would have to deal with the benefits he was receiving from not changing those of receiving sympathy and all the pity he got for his "struggles." That itself would have been helpful.

If it is a financial theme, it should be realistic but hurt. For some people, "hurt" is $500. For others it's $10,000. This is a judgment call. In our experience if there is a sharp inhale of breath when discussing the number, it's just about right. But penalties don't always have to be about money. I have used the technique of a penalty a number of times with other, more creative approaches. With one overweight client, for instance, who had historically wanted to exercise but could never "find the time" in his busy day, the penalty was to clean his ex-wife's house once a week for a year. He would have rather died than miss his goal of weight loss and daily aerobics. Today, forty pounds lighter and with a healthier body, he attributes this creative penalty as the essential help needed for breakthrough.

Randori teaches us to be judicious when using the penalty approach. If done for the wrong reason, it can be punishing, only reinforcing a self-view of failure. It's very important to make sure the intention of "penalty" is to support the individual. A trusting relationship is essential. Without it, you will be perceived as cruel or manipulative. But at the right time and place with the right person it can be a powerful technique for breaking through stubborn and long-standing intransigence.

Reference

Hall, C. S., & Lindzey, G. (1978). *Theories of Personality, 3e*, New York: John Wiley & Sons.

A Long Time or a Short Time?

Carol A. Erickson

A young lady came to my office seeking help with a problem that she considered to be very serious. She announced that she was frigid and had been so for quite a while and that she didn't know what to do about it. As a therapist I began to ask her a number of questions and discovered that she had been married for about eight years and that at this time she and her husband were living like roommates. She informed me that they were friends and that they each had separate bedrooms and that they never shared a communal bed. They did not have arguments about this situation. It was by mutual agreement. She stated that she enjoyed the friendship with him, but did not feel that they had a real marriage and she wanted a real marriage. She thought that he was not interested in being with her in an intimate relationship, and she felt the same way in regard to him. After approaching this subject in a variety of ways, I asked the young woman how she knew she was frigid. She looked at me in an astonished way, and stated "he told me I was," meaning of course, her husband. I asked if that was the sole basis on which she made the decision that she was frigid. She answered, "of course."

I began to explore with her how she felt about expanding her social life and if she really wished to stay married to this man. After a good bit of discussion, it became clear that she was feeling lonely and desired more social interaction. It also became quite clear that she was not committed to maintaining the marriage, as in her mind it was really over. She also told me that he had made similar statements to the effect that he thought that the marriage was over, too. I inquired as to whether he would be jealous if she began to have some social life on her own. She stated no, and that he had even encouraged her to go out with her friends and have some fun. At that point, I talked with her about the necessity sometimes of getting second opinions about serious conditions, and she asked me if I knew of someone to whom I could refer her. I asked her if she knew any friendly single people at her work. She said that there were several. I suggested that she invite both males and females separately to go to lunch with her and begin to build up some new friendships.

She again asked me about referring her for a second opinion, and I told her that she needed to do the socializing first, and that then I would give her a good referral. Also, I encouraged her to go on dates with the new friends if that should come up. I told her at this point that I did not want to go into more detail about her problem, and that the homework of socializing needed to occur first. I booked another appointment with her for about three weeks later. I told her that she could call me at any time if there were any changes or she needed to consult.

Approximately two weeks later, I got a phone call from an extremely excited young female whose voice I recognized. Fortunately, I did recognize it, since she forgot to even tell me who was calling, because she was so excited to share her results with me. She said, "I'm not! I'm not!" laughing gaily. She then informed me that she did not need to come for another appointment. I laughed with her and encouraged her to go out and explore her life. I also briefly discussed with her that she really needed to address completion with her husband. She indicated she realized the marriage was over, that she had spoken with him, and they had agreed to do a no fault dissolution. She did complete the divorce and later established a satisfying relationship with a new husband.

Successful short-term therapy is a gift and a blessing to the client, the therapist, and the community. Everybody has a story, and all of us get caught in limiting boxes or frames of references, some of our own making. It's wonderful to have a "box" or stuck place open up so quickly, and with minimal negative side effects and lots of new positive possibilities. Life is too short to stay in rigid stuck places and, as we know, the clock is always ticking.

Prostate Cancer as a Sporting Event

castigated by my sister I'm told
Never to refer to it again as
"My cancer."
and "Helpline Harry" says
I'm the captain of the ship
in other words in this house
I hold the channel changer
right now I'm on Channel 9
running the marathon
a race in which it matters not
how quick you came off the blocks
what matters is keeping pace
and possessing a finishing kick
blistering hot

Click—over to basketball
not a sport for short people
hell, when I was forty
I was already so far behind I decided
there and then that winning the game
is not what's important
what is important though
is that I look good while losing

Click—football is a world of hurt
knocks and hits

and playing through the pain
to a place in the game
where we're five points down
with seconds to go
a "never say die" situation
the old flea flicker—I let the ball fly..

Click—over to a baseball
of late my favorite sport
played on a diamond in a field of grass
bleachers, sunshine and always
the possibility of extra innings
theoretically
the contest can last forever
but reality being what reality is
one day the arm will tire
with Sammy Sosa at the plate
on deck Mark McGuire

Click—back to the Hail Mary
me streaking down the field
faking out the linebacker
catching the ball
I fall in the end zone
game over—game won
the fans in the stands Irish waking

Click—"If you've just tuned in,
it's the top of the tenth
with the score tied at eight all."
the umpire dusts off the plate
"Batter up." he shouts
"Play ball!"

Ric Masten

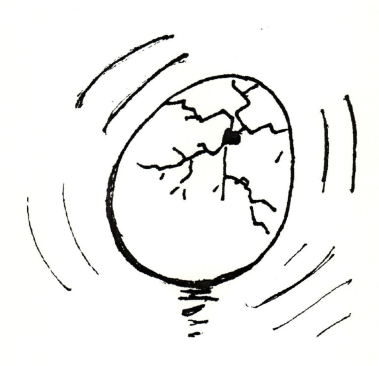

On the Banks of the Ohio

Phil Ziegler

It was the mid-70s. An exciting time to be entering the mental health field. In fact, there was some question about whether it should be called the mental health field. What we were part of was the "human potential movement"; we were interested in people's strengths and in exploring the limits of human consciousness and possibility, not so much in curing mental illness. (My solution-oriented, strength-based roots go deep.) I had been practicing law, but was not happy in that profession. I went into group therapy and immediately recognized—as did the leaders and other group members—that I had a natural flare for therapy work. When I was ready to leave the group, the leaders, well-known family therapists, offered to train me as a lay family therapist. I jumped at the opportunity and eventually got a position as a paraprofessional counselor in a community-based youth and family program.

As the program went through a series of changes, expanding, reorganizing, redesigning itself, I moved up to the position of clinical director. I went back to graduate school, earned an MA, and, by the time I got my degree, I had a staff of eight licensed clinicians working under me. I was responsible for training and supervising them. In addition, because conjoint family therapy was still relatively new, I was regularly being invited to provide in-service training to social service and mental health agencies around the San Francisco Bay Area. All this went to my head—I was somebody important, somebody the profession was noticing.

But, I was not very happy or satisfied. For one thing, while I was a pretty good therapist and trainer, I was a terrible administrator. To make matters worse, the agency director was even less effective. So, while to the outside world the agency appeared to be a model program, inside, staff morale was low and we were spending more and more time dealing with in-house problems than we were delivering services to the community.

My wife, my friends, my therapist, my staff and a lot of other people were working hard to convince me that I needed to leave the agency. I agreed, but stayed on giving them and myself one reason after another why I had to stay a few more months. Talk about stuck. I was like the proverbial monkey caught in the coconut trap—I couldn't break free because I couldn't let go of the piece of food. I just couldn't let go even though holding on was doing me a lot of harm.

In the middle of this, I got a call from Jan, an old college friend, a musician I used to play and sing with. (As will become clear in a moment, I loved sitting around someone's apartment singing and playing guitar, but I hated stage performance and rarely performed publicly.) He now had a music school, and every year the school had a music and performance camp. He invited me to come to the camp as his guest. I told him I'd love to come so long as I didn't have to perform in public. He assured me the choice was mine, I could sit in on the workshops and just attend performance night.

My wife and I arrived and found there were about 100 people at the camp. The teaching staff was of the highest caliber—Bobby McFarrin (relatively unknown at that time) was there along with some of the top jazz and blues musicians in the San Francisco Bay Area. The camp was structured so that participants took workshops for two days in preparation for the final evening, at which time everyone had the opportunity to perform, using whatever and whomever they wanted as backup.

I'd love to be able to tell you that Bobby McFarrin and I did a duet, singing a song I wrote during a song writing workshop entitled, "Don't worry, be happy." But, it would be a lie. What did happen is that another old friend of mine, Ray, who was at the camp, convinced me that he and I should get up on performance night and just sing one of the folk songs we used to sing in the old days. "Just for the fun of it," Ray said. And, I agreed. For the next two days, I grew increasingly anxious about having foolishly agreed to play guitar and sing, "On the Banks of the Ohio" in front of over 100 serious performers.

On performance night, it turned out there were about 60 acts—7 hours worth of them. Ray and I were the 59th act on the list. So, for 7 hours I watched and listened to singer after singer, one backup band and backup vocal group after another. I kept asking myself, "How the hell did I get into this?" "How can I get out of this?" I kept coming up with ideas: "I know, I'll just tell Jan I'm sick and can't perform." "Maybe if I just cross our names off the list, no one will notice or give a damn. Hell, Ray can get up there on his own if he wants." I started testing people out by mentioning I was thinking it might be best if we didn't perform, pointing out that there were so many acts and making the point that Ray and I weren't really serious performers anyway. But everyone kept saying it would be a lot of fun, a great experience, and a chance to show what I could do. That coconut trap, again? So I didn't cross our names off that long list and my anxiety continued to grow more intense as act after act did their thing.

About 3:00 in the morning, the last acts were having their few moments in the limelight. Finally, after the longest night of my life, our time arrived. Ray and I stepped onto the stage. My knees were shaking, my fingers frozen. Looking out toward the audience, I could hear people but I couldn't see a soul—the spotlight kept everyone in the dark. I put the sheet of paper with the words and chords down on the music stand, pulled a chair over, put my foot up on it, placed the guitar on my thigh. Ray and I leaned toward the microphone. It was then that I noticed that the spotlight was positioned so I couldn't see the page with the words and chords. And, my fingers still wouldn't move when I tried to pluck the guitar strings. My heart was pounding so hard there was no way I could sing—I could hardly talk. Sheer terror. My worst performance nightmare. Ray nodded to me to start playing, but I just stood there not moving, staring at the page I couldn't see.

Then all of a sudden I started to speak. Well, more like I'm listening to someone else, but knowing it's me talking into the microphone. I hear myself say, "I'm here tonight to demonstrate performance anxiety." Some laughter in the audience. "See these fingers…frozen. They will not move. It's weird—I am telling them to move but they won't obey." More laughter. I am beginning to relax now, actually enjoying the moment. "Anybody know the words to *The Banks of the Ohio*?" I ask. "You can sing along if you like. In fact, you can come up here and if you can get this damned guitar out of my hands, you can play it and sing it yourself." More laughter. Now, I want to see everyone. I ask that the spotlight be turned off. With the spotlight off I can see that the audience is loving it. People are slapping their knees, doubling over with laughter, thoroughly enjoying whatever the hell it is I'm doing. I sense it's time to end and turn to Ray. I strum the guitar once, nod toward him, and together we sing only one phrase, "On the banks….of the O-Hi-O." We bow. The audience is on its feet. We're getting a rousing standing ovation—we're a hit. I am in a state of shock.

The camp ended on Sunday. The following Monday morning I was sitting in a staff meeting and suddenly heard myself announce, to my own surprise, that I had decided to leave the agency, that I would stay on one more month to help find a replacement clinical director. I left a month later and rented some office space part time. My private practice, I am happy to say, grew quickly and has provided good support for my family and me for over 25 years.

Getting Unstuck from Life's Calamities in Five Easy Steps

Phoebe Prosky

Calamities don't happen to us; we create them by the fearful thoughts or thwarted expectations we bring to our experiences. Here's a way to literally change your mind so you can see events clearly and avoid calamities.

1. Decide on a length of time for this practice (1 minute, ½ hour as you wish).

2. Sit cross-legged on the floor on the edge of a fat pillow or in a chair, with your back straight but not rigid.

3. Take your attention to your breath. With your mind's eye, observe the rise and fall of your abdomen. (This quiets thoughts.)

4. When your mind wanders from this focus, gently bring it back and begin observing your breath again.

5. Continue this practice for the time you decided upon at the outset.

There is no failing at this. A wandering mind gives you more practice in bringing your attention back to the breath. You may feel some relaxation the first time you practice or perhaps not for many times. Eventually your mind will learn to let go of anything you ask it to. Then you can see clearly without the intercession of fear or expectation. You will encounter no calamities.

(Optimal breathing requires that breathing be abdominal. When we breathe in, our abdomen expands to enlarge the space for our lungs to fill; when we breathe out, our abdomen compresses, exhaling air from the very bottom of the lungs up. Our shoulders do not move at all in optimal breathing.)

A Time To Refocus

Fred P. Piercy

The motivational speaker was on a roll.

"I have a plan to sail around the world in three years," he said. "I even have a picture of the sailboat I want with a little picture of me at the helm."

He told each of us to believe in ourselves, to identify our long-term goals, and to never give up until we reached them.

As he spoke, I wondered how his message was playing to his audience, many of whom were living with cancer. What were their long-term goals and how did the sailboat relate to them?

Of course, there's a time to work toward grand dreams. But when serious illness hits, most of us learn to live more in the present, and to let go of goals that seemed a lot more important before we got sick. Perhaps the audience could have taught the motivational speaker a thing or two about living in the shadow of death.

Colleague Shobha Pais and I studied how people with AIDS make sense of their disease and how the meaning they give it helps them cope.

Most see life a lot differently since they've gotten sick.

"Every little thing has so much more meaning," says one AIDS patient. Another says, "I get up every morning and I thank God Almighty that I have this day to live."

Faced with death, people look for meaning in various places. Some find it in relationships, or in caring for a sick partner, or even in caring for a pet. Others find meaning in God or the lessons they learn—patience, humility, perspective, love—as they slog through another day.

Dr. Froma Walsh, from the University of Chicago, has studied how strong families get through serious illness and death.

"Many resilient families try to make sense out of the challenges they face." Walsh says. "Whether or not they can change their situation, they tend to stay positive and see a larger purpose. Many reconnect with their faith."

According to Walsh, resilient families support one another and reach out to family and the community for support. They aren't afraid to express all their feelings—sadness, happiness, grief. Clearly, we can learn a lot from people facing death. In the popular book, *Tuesdays with Morrie*, dying Morrie Schwartz tells his young friend, Mitch, about a Buddhist practice of picturing a bird on your shoulder whispering, "Is today the day you will die? Are you ready? Is today the day?" Maybe we all need a bird on our shoulders to remind us of the preciousness of the moment, the short time we have to do good, and to show those close to us that we care.

I recently asked a client couple who felt disconnected from one another whether, if they had cancer, their partner would be there for them. Both agreed that their partner would indeed rally around them in their time of need. "If you would do it then, why not now?" I asked.

Ghandi once said, "Each night when I go to sleep, I die. And each morning when I wake up, I am reborn." Each of us starts a new day each morning, and each of us is given one more chance to get it right, while there's still time.

I guess there's nothing wrong with working toward a sailboat, if you want to. Just remember that bird on your shoulder as you do.

LEE BERER

Good Days/Bad Days

In turn, I've met them all
Doctors Slash, Poison, & Burn

on good days
my urologist is Arthur of Camelot
wielding Excalibur in my defense
Zorro, foiling enemy lesions
a deft dashing master of surgery
on bad days—Jack the Ripper!
stropping an edge on his flashing blade
Sweeney Todd intent on doing butchery
Genghis Khan hacking and chopping
his way through me

on good days
my oncologist is Merlin wise and kind
dispenser of healing elixirs
the Lone Ranger coming to the rescue
leaving silver bullets behind
on bad days—Dr. Jeckyl!
with unexpected side effects to Hyde
like the cackling witch in Snow White
he stirs his bubbling cauldron
feeding me apples with venom inside

on good days
my radiologist is Keeper of the Fire
Shaman—squire of healing beams

firing off therapeutic volleys
the Buck Rogers of my dreams
on bad days—Dr. Strangelove!
fondling his arsenal of bombs
Nero fiddling fanning the flames
and if General Sherman is on the march
then Georgia is my name

in closing
I suppose it's obvious
and goes without my having to say
that these contrary lines were composed
on a very
very bad day

Ric Masten

Tools for Getting Unstuck

John Frykman

I'm a "talker," not really a "writer," but write I must, and that's difficult for me. I find myself procrastinating, using every trick in the book to avoid doing what I really need and want to do. It's part of what has motivated me to share ideas that I have developed over many years of working as a psychotherapist, minister, community organizer—ideas, strategies, and methods for "Getting Unstuck." Some will seem goofy, others "tried and true," but all of them are examples of "things that have worked" for many people in a huge variety of life situations. They spring from the mind and experience of one who is a "helper/facilitator/coach" but they are pretty much accessible, transferable, and useful to a wide range of people who want to get unstuck.

My tools are divided into three categories:

1. Helpful Principles

2. Examples and Stories

3. Maximizing Chances for Success

A few examples to get us started:

You've been feeling blue, life is starting to seem hopeless. The "committee" of voices is buzzing in your head. You feel yourself being pulled down through the funnel cloud of the tornado of your own mind. Get on the phone, call someone, anyone. A clerk in a store, a friend, family member, make reservations for a play, whatever. Just get out of your head and things will begin to move.

Can't get started on paying bills. You're "mustificating" (a lá Albert Ellis), must do this, must do that. Your chest is getting tighter and tighter. Gather all the materials that you need to do the job and put them in one accessible place. The bills, checkbook, records. Then make a decision that sometime later that very day you are going to go to that place and spend just fifteen minutes working on the bills, no matter how little or how much you get done during that time. At the end of the time, consciously decide: "Am I going to work on these bills any longer or not?" If the answer is, "Yes," decide how many more minutes you are going to work on them. "OK, it's going pretty well, I'll work on them for thirty more minutes." At the end of that period, stop, set a "next time" that you will come back to work on them, write it in your appointment book, and then do something nice to reward yourself for a job well done. If the answer is, "No," stop immediately, set a time to come back to it the next day for another fifteen minute period, then go do something you enjoy to give yourself credit for the fifteen minutes you have already put into the project. Each time you come back to the task, follow the same procedure until the job is complete.

You've been biting your nails. They look awful. You've tried EVERYTHING you can think of to stop. You've put nasty tasting stuff on them. You've put band-aids on them all. You have worn gloves, tied one hand behind your back, on and on. Instead, try something new; all of the above are proven failures anyhow. Choose just one of your fingers on which you will focus. You are going to care for that one finger and its fingernail. You will keep it clean, use a special polish on it, make it your friend. Maybe you will never be able to stop biting your nails but you will be able to care for this one special nail. Don't pay any attention to any of the other nails. Do whatever you want with them. When your special nail is clear and beautiful and you can look at it with pride, choose another nail to care for. Sooner than you think, you'll find all of your nails are beautiful and you will have created a solution that applies to many other things in your life.

Is your imagination getting going?

Helpful Principles

As a helping person, I've learned that success is in the details. I can't expect the people I work with to get with who I am; it's my job to get with who they are, whether it's an individual, couple, or family.

Dress Code: At our first meeting I normally wear a coat, shirt, and tie. It's a way of showing respect. Who knows if the person might be very uncomfortable if I showed up in jeans and a sweatshirt? I can always take the coat and tie off; it's very difficult to put them on. The point is, I want to be able to use all the resources I have for the benefit of those I serve. When I was working as a minister I almost always wore a black clergy shirt and clerical collar—it was a mark of who I was.

Don't these same principles transfer to what one wears when applying for a job, going on a first date, attending a picnic, meeting someone for the first time?

Collaboration: Another key word for me is collaboration. I want to work WITH people, not talk down or up to them. In my private practice, when someone calls to make a first appointment, I offer a brief first session without charge so that they can meet me, learn how I work, decide if they want to work with me, ask questions, in other words, if we begin, we have a contract to collaborate from the start. I'm not there to tell them what to do, give them easy answers, but to work together towards a solution.

Respect: Respect is key. I'm not one to try to make someone over into a clone of me, that I have the right way to live life and they don't. I want to help them develop solutions that grow out of their own values and ways of living, not mine. "Different strokes for different folks" is something I live by.

Note Taking: Whether working to help someone else or helping yourself, taking notes is vital in keeping on track and creating a picture of what needs to be done. When you take notes, your unconscious mind is connected to your writing hand as well as your conscious. When you review your notes, there are often surprises, surprises that turn into keys to solution. The notes provide a graphic picture, a road map of where you are headed and where you have been in your thinking and strategizing.

Mining Resources: Getting unstuck is a process of mining resources. What does this person bring to the table that can be used to help them get unstuck? We all have hidden resources that we have never used, in some cases, resources that we thought were liabilities. One of my most important teachers, Milton H. Erickson, M.D., once used the skill a young man had of squirting water accurately between his two front teeth as an asset that landed him a wife and family and the happiness that had long evaded him.

Efficiency: Efficiency is another important principle. Sessions on solutions need only be as long as they need be—not just 45 or 50 minute sessions. Some sessions might last but a few minutes, others might last an hour-and-a-half. I leave the possibility of two hours for a first session—I need to take the time to learn how it is in the life of the person or family I'm working with.

Quantity of Information: Quantity of information is also important. I want to respect the privacy of my client's life. If I don't need a lot of ancient history, I don't go looking for it. What is it that is necessary to know, that is happening here and now, moving us toward concrete solutions, and not one word more?

Proven Failures: In finding ways to get unstuck, it's very important to gather a list of "Attempted Solutions." What have I already tried in order to get myself moving? What you thus gather is a list of failed solutions, which one does not want to try again; they are proven failures. "More of the same" is not going to be better. "I took two aspirin for a headache and it didn't work, so I took two more," etc., "and finally my stomach started bleeding."

No Advice: And finally, the principle of not giving advice is so important. When we give advice, we are usually offering something to someone else that has worked for us. It most likely is not going to work for them. Their situation, relationships, and resources are different and what is going to work for them needs to grow out of their life and their resources.

In a nutshell, it's taking all of the person's resources seriously. It's respecting them, respecting yourself, building strategies for change that grow out of the uniqueness of a person's life, strategies that are action plans, not changed attitudes or understandings. Too many are all too sure of the reasons for their "stuckness" and remain in the muck and mire of inability to make the changes they want for their lives. So often, it's not the problem that is the problem, but what one is doing about the problem. So if what you are doing to get unstuck is not working, change what you are doing.

Examples and Stories

"I don't know."

He sat in the chair, a chunk of a 14 year old. His mother sat beside him. She seemed exhausted, beside herself. As we gathered information the only words from Peter were, "I dunno," again and again, no matter what the topic. She spilled out the problems at school, problems with friends, problems with getting up in the morning, problems going to bed at night, problems, problems, problems. It was very difficult to find any resources coming from them that could be used for a plan.

"Maybe this situation is hopeless. Maybe there is nothing we can come up with together that's going to help."

Mom: "I think I've tried everything." Peter: "I dunno."

"There is one thing that you seem able to do, Peter. No matter what is said or asked, you are able to respond with, 'I dunno.' Perhaps that has a little glimmer of some change in it. Would you be willing to try something, Peter, even if it seems not much different than what you are already doing, just to see if anything is possible?"

"I dunno," he said, beginning to smile and perk up just a little.

"What about you, Mom, are you willing to enter into a little experiment that might seem a little silly, off the wall?"

"OK, what can it hurt, it can't be any worse than it already is."

"Peter, what I'd like to suggest is that you keep doing what you are already doing but do it in a little bit different way. Instead of saying 'I dunno' every time you're spoken to, would you be willing to say the same thing but just a bit more intentionally, instead of, 'I dunno,' say, 'I—DON'T—KNOW' slowly and clearly pronounced." (He was grinning a little "I know what you're up to" smirk.)

"I dunno, ah, I mean, I—DON'T—KNOW."

The three of us starting laughing and almost couldn't stop. "I think when I see you again that you both will have an amazing story to tell." And they did.

Lessons from Uncle Milty (Milton H. Erickson, M.D.)

Dr. Erickson was one of my most important teachers. For several years I made journeys to be with him in Phoenix, Arizona, and learn from him. He was a psychiatrist and a pioneer in the fields of psychotherapy, hypnosis, and dealing with problems in a highly individualistic and efficient way. Therapy did not have to take years of four-times-a-week visits. In fact, for many, one or two sessions were all that was needed. He was the only therapist that I have ever known that seemed to know exactly what to suggest in every situation that presented itself to him. What follows are just a few fascinating things that I learned from him that illustrate the importance of noticing details and tailoring any approach to an exact situation. They also highlight some of the commonalities we have as human beings.

Healing Stories

Lighting the Fire (one of my own stories)

As you are telling me of your troubles, I'm remembering a story I once told my wife.

Lying here beside you, my thoughts wander over the many times we have shared space together (warm). So often I think of times when we have built a beautiful fire together in the (warm) fireplace. Finding the paper for the base, crumpling it up, just so, and placing it on the grate (warm). Looking for just the right (warm) kindling wood, short pieces, dry, fragile, fragrant. Stacking them (warm) in the beautiful way we have done so many times before, just the same (warm) but always so new and fresh. Looking for the larger pieces of wood and carefully making a tepee of them over the kindling foundation. Feeling the excitement (warm) build as I reach for the matches, strike one and watch it (warm) flare, then touching it to paper, first here, then there, and again up higher (warm). Loving the flush that comes as the fire begins to burst (warm) forth. Hearing the crackle of the wood as the intensity grows. Finally lifting (warm) the larger logs and setting them on (warm) the burning tepee, loving the sensation in our very soul as the logs are encircled and (warm) begin to glow.

Now, you can go home and build your OWN fire. You can help warm each other and it can be your fire and yours alone. A special experience, like no other in the world. Perhaps you will share your experience when I see you again. And what is it that you are thinking about, *N O W!*

Surprising Meanings

"Dr. Erickson, several times I have heard you say, seemingly out of the blue with no clues given to you by the patient, 'does your husband know about the affair you've been having?' How in the world do you know that the woman has been having an affair?"

"When the patient sits down at the beginning of treatment, crosses her legs, then tucks the toe of the one leg behind the calf of the other, I know. It's never failed to be so in all the times I have noticed it and asked the question." (This writer has checked this out on several occasions and can corroborate this story.)

Milton Erickson was the consummate observer, looking for clues in what the patient was bringing to treatment that could be used to help the person achieve goals.

Another example of this was when he would decide on rare occasions that a patient was impossible to help. I asked him how he could tell. "When you are talking to such a person it is very difficult to get their attention. They will not want to look you in the eye. They will be answering your questions before the question is even finished. They are the 'me' baby, at the center of the whole universe, wanting the universe to attend to their every need. (In AA they call this the King Baby syndrome.) Very simply, they are stuck in a rigid box and allow nothing in. They live within a closed system. I know they will not be responsive to my suggestions and so do not continue to work with them."

In my own life, when I've found it difficult to change and have needed to, I've asked myself, "Am I putting myself in an unbreakable box, unable to open up and do the things necessary to change?" And many times I have.

Amplification

One final example of my learnings from "Uncle Milty" is his concept of amplification. Instead of going for the "whole solution," Dr. Erickson would often look for small, even infinitesimal movement, then amplify that movement. (See fingernail illustration above.) Another example was told to me by one of my clients:

"As a little guy, I was one of the multitude who got into carrying my 'blankie' (cotton flannel security blanket) wherever I went. I couldn't be without it. One morning when I awakened, I noticed that my blankie was half the size it was when I went to bed, but, I still had it so it was O.K. A few days later it was half that size, and later half that size, and so forth and so on, until I had but a very small remnant of the blankie and I realized I didn't need to have it at all anymore. I threw that last bit away, all by myself. My dear mother had developed a clever way to take it away without taking it 'away' that helped me get unstuck from my need for that blanket."

Maximizing Chances for Success

Begin with the basic idea that the only person that you can control is yourself. We waste so much time and energy in our futile attempts to control others. This is not to say there's nothing that can be done. There are many options and strategies that can lift us out of our stuck places to more satisfying realities in our lives. If you change what you are doing in any stuck situation, the situation will change. It won't necessarily get better right away, but it will change. And the new situation, even if it seems worse at the beginning, is easier to modify than the one that has kept you captive for such a long time. If what you are doing to "help" your situation is not helping you to change, it is not "help."

Sometimes clients are amazed at ideas that I suggest to them, not realizing that the very idea that is being suggested is coming from information that they have given to me. Once you become aware of the many options that are possible, you will be able to come up with new coping strategies yourself. Too often people think in terms of it's either "this or that," when in reality there are hundreds of choices or alternatives between the extremes of this or that. Let me share a few to stimulate your imagination.

Past Box. Allowing the past to control what's happening to you now? Difficult childhood, broken relationships, never finished college, etc. Get a shoe box (or any manageable size container you like) and decorate it nicely. In large letters on the outside write, "THE PAST." Every time one of those troublesome thoughts of self condemnations from the past comes up, write it down on a scrap of paper, and when you have the opportunity, put it in the box, saying (preferably out loud), "I can put this in THE PAST and leave it there." Some time later, when you are no longer plagued by the past, you can arrange a burial or cremation of the box and finally and fully bury the past, making the choice to no longer allow the past to control your life now.

Handling Criticism. Have trouble when someone criticizes you? "You're never on time." "You always treat me badly." "Don't you ever follow through?" Start by changing the way you respond to the criticism. Perhaps: "Maybe you're right. Do you have any ideas for me?" You don't have to agree or disagree, or get defensive, try to win an argument, you simply move yourself into a position of power by allowing the person's point of view. After all, the other side of "maybe you're right" is "maybe you're wrong!" Another example: "Why don't you ever put the toilet seat down?" Response: "I don't really know why. Could you help me with that?" In relationships, "why" questions are poison. They don't really mean, "Why?" They mean, "justify yourself," forcing defensiveness. Nobody really asks, "Why are you home on time?" It's almost always, "Why are you late?"

Couples Communication. Need to feel safer talking about intimate things with your partner? Try a "10 and 10" every day for a week or more if necessary. Pick a time when you will not be interrupted. Honor that time as a sacred island of time set aside for the two of you. Sit together in a quiet place. Each of you should have a spiral notebook and pen or pencil. Be sure the telephone is unplugged and cell phones and pagers are turned off, no one else is around or expected to be coming round to disturb your tranquility. Then, for ten minutes, write about what you are feeling (1) about yourself, (2) about your partner, (3) about your relationship. It doesn't matter how much or how little you write, just that you stop at the end of ten minutes. Then exchange notebooks with each other. Read what your partner has written. Then for ten minutes, discuss what you have written. One partner facilitates the discussion, the next session, the other facilitates, and so on. At the end of ten minutes, STOP. "Ten and ten" is a process to make personal communication more and more safe. Trust the process. Even if your discussion is animated and fun, stop, keep to the plan until you get to the place when you know that you can talk about even the most intimate things, deeply and safely.

Goodbye Letters and Things Related. In the fellowship of Alcoholics Anonymous, there are many rituals and pithy sayings. A few of them that have genuine relevance to the process of getting unstuck are:

> "Fake it 'til you make it." Sometimes all you need to do is pretend to be able to do something long enough, and it does become possible. "I can't stand up and give a speech, so I'll pretend that I can and do it anyway."

> When some one asks you, "How are you doing?" and you respond, "Fine." "Fine" really means, "*F*ouled up, *I*nsecure, *N*eurotic, and *E*motional." In other words, it isn't usually helpful to minimize how difficult something is.

> "Easy Does It." Flexibility is important in getting unstuck and on track. Black and white thinking leads to rigidity and "terminal uniqueness."

> (See "Alcoholics Anonymous'" latest edition for many more wonderful aids to recovery and getting unstuck.)

Writing "goodbye letters" that are not really meant to be mailed but part of a process are often very helpful. For example, a letter to someone who has died without your having a chance to communicate your care or unfinished business with them. A letter to Alcohol or Cocaine or Marijuana…A letter to an abusive parent…To a lost friend. A letter written in "invisible ink" and actually sent to a person that has meant much pain in your life. It can be one, two, as many pages as you like, and you can "imagine" that you have written everything that you have ever wanted to say to that person but have been afraid to say. It can give a person a chance to get thoughts out of the head, the mind, down on paper, and be very helpful in moving on with life, past grief or loss or resentment, etc.

From many sources comes a truism: The past is over, the future is yet to come, but the present is a gift. So much of being stuck is allowing the past or future to dominate one's present reality in often debilitating ways.

Power objects. In my counseling office I have many objects that can be useful in helping people to get unstuck. They include timers, bells, beads, pedometers, beatle clickers, rosaries, hour glasses, talismans, costume jewelry, pins, many, many things. Things often contribute power that facilitates change. Timeouts can be measured by a three-minute timer. It's easier to "walk until the pedometer reads two miles" than to guess at what you are accomplishing. "Worry beads" can be passed through fingers in conjunction with controlled breathing when anxiety rears its head. A wife can silently pass her husband a small ceramic dove, when she feels he is starting to act in inappropriate ways at a public event. A friend can click a clicker every time the person he is trying to help does a certain unwanted behavior. When a person touches a large, special ceremonial coin in his pocket, he can remember what he is choosing to do rather than continuing to do what he has always done. A teenager can count the number of times (on a pocket counter) an unreasonable parent says "no" to reasonable requests and learn that almost always there will be a yes after five no's. And on and on.

Finally. Another of my important teachers, Saul David Alinski, said once: "Peace is not the absence of conflict but the restoration of community." Peace is really a sense of wholeness, that the fragmented parts of our lives are beginning to fit together. That's what getting unstuck from life's calamities, troubles, vexations is about. Not that we have everything nailed down but that we have the freedom of feeling that we are unstuck, that we are on the path moving toward a goal. It's not already being at the goal that makes things OK, but the sense that we are on the way.

The Narratives We Weave Sometimes Need Unraveling

Timothy F. Dwyer

One autumn evening my wife, Laura and I were entertaining some new friends, Tom and Liz. This was a couple that we had just met a few weeks earlier, when Tom was hired to work in my department. We'd already finished dinner and repaired to the living room with coffee and dessert when we began sharing stories of our lives and some critical incidents of our growing up.

I'd begun to tell the story of my father's exit and virtual absence from my family. It was a familiar tale I'd become quite skilled in telling. I had told this story many times and I think Laura began to hear it more clearly for what I didn't tell. You see, I had become so versed in this tale that it was predictable to her. She knew what points I'd punctuate for dramatic flair, she saw how I'd turn a phrase to create just the right touch of sentimental poignancy and balance of humor that would clearly convey my intended themes of resilience and acceptance. Initially, she heard the story as a cogent and well-narrated package, one which left few questions open or dangling to the average listener. I told it in a way that always managed to cast me in a certain light that was rather heroic for my young tender years, and at the same time portrayed me as a well put together young man who had suffered such a tragic loss and could tell it so eloquently now. It was a story of inspiration, a story of acceptance, a story of loss and love and redemption. Who could not be moved by such a story?

So here I was this particular evening telling my well-honed tale and our new friends were showing the rapt attention I'd come to anticipate, when I glanced over to Laura and noticed her looking puzzled and piqued. She gave me an incredulous and dubious look, but was polite enough to not interrupt my seamless narrative. It was too late, however. I was distracted and lost my focus. I quickly tied up the loose ends of my story, foregoing the neat and tidy ribbon that would have left my listeners little choice but to exclaim with sympathy, tenderness and just a touch of awe, "Oh, Tim, what a powerful and moving story."

No, that night's telling had a different ending and for me it signaled a messy beginning.

After I'd concluded my truncated story, I looked at Laura and asked, "what's the matter?" She did not hesitate at my invitation. She began, "you know, I've heard this story a number of times and I've never said anything before, but I just find it hard to believe that this man, your dad, who was so beloved by all who knew him, and was so well-known, was able to drop completely out of sight under the noses of everyone. I just find it hard to believe that no one knew where he was all that time. I mean, what's strange to me is that no one questioned this. No one looked for him. No one had any contact. No one...." she continued for several minutes to mine the void with laser precision and ask all the unasked questions I'd skillfully, unobtrusively skated around. My face felt hot and I was convinced it looked like red chili pepper. I was in a panic with a mixture of rage and embarrassment. My first thought was, "How dare you! How dare you cast this shadow on my light, cast aspersion on my tale of redemption." More than anything, she poked holes in this pretty package, this boxed up story I'd kept like a sacred family symbol, revered and presented as archival truth.

In the moment Laura tore into the package I felt a mixture of anger, fear, and sadness. The show was over. It was time to grow up. My capacity for ambiguity grew in that moment. Not that I didn't want to throttle Laura at first. A part of me wanted to lash back, to say, "Fuck you! You don't know my family." I felt the crushing weight of all my family myths bearing down and calling on me to defend all the *Dwyers*. "Moreover, at this moment my dear wife, you are clearly NOT a *Dwyer*." I thought, "shame on you for not supporting the myth!"

Masterfully and with the grace of some god no doubt, I contained my impulse. I took a breath and then another. I wiped the rage and embarrassment from my eyes to see that Laura was not attacking me. There was a softness in her face, a tenderness that was unmistakable. Though she still held the scissors, the wrapping of my package pulled back to reveal a tattered box. Her look told me she was coming from a loving place. And without another word her look said to me, "it's okay to open this up, to look inside and see how the contents have shifted. Its time to look and see what parts still fit and which don't, which parts need repair, and what parts are missing. Trust me. I will help you look for those that are missing."

Laura took a risk, a big risk, to unravel my narrative. She raised my anxiety and she challenged me to grow. You see, it had been years since that box was open. It had been years since I wrapped it up and found the great joy and satisfaction in showing it off in its decorated style. In the telling, I would allude to what the story contained, but the contents of the box remained concealed, even to me. While the illusion was presented in my narrative so clearly and so beautifully, its mystery was obstructed. Laura was absolutely right to ask those questions. She compelled me to step back and look at my story in a new light. As a result, I began to ask my own questions. I might add, I raised the anxiety of a few of my family members in that process. I remember my Mom saying to me when I presented her with my newly opened box of questions, "Tim, I'm just afraid that you might find out something that you won't want to know." I couldn't imagine what that might be and I have a pretty good imagination.

I learned then that sometimes our boxes need to be reopened, our narratives need a little unraveling. Since that time I've come to open myself to a process that has allowed me—to paraphrase T.S. Eliot—to see my history, and to tell it, as though it were the very first time. Now, each time I tell my tale I feel myself different. Now, I am more able to see facets and to mine narratives I had not considered before. Now, I am more able to leave the box open and a little untidy. I welcome the questions such as Laura's because I see in them possibilities of not diminishing but enlarging my box to contain new stories always unfolding.

Tai Chi with Catherine

sunrise—sunset
I gaze at the horizon
breath sweeps mind

the ancient wheel
an old man works
weeping with joy

ocean currents
the dark slow dance of kelp
a glimpse of stars

sea waves
a wash of reflected sky
stolen footprints

slow flight
the expression of frustration
tempo...largo

daughter on the mountain
tends her greenery
the faint scent of sage

daughter in the valley
blanket of snow
and a tea kettle singing

seasons of change
the sympathy of maple trees
mirror image

the tides
laden with treasure
a hand written note

renewal
midway between dawn and dusk
peanut butter sandwiches

two rivers meet
together
they leave Pittsburgh

the waterfall
against her misty apron
a bird in flight

the winding river
from the window seat
a long lazy blue ribbon
where the river meets the sea
in the froth of confusion
steelhead leap

light in the hidden temple
a line of pilgrims
shadow dancing

silent strength
pushing against the stillness
giving way

golden journey
coins spill brightly
from hand to hand

passing clouds
and the billow of sheets
prayers in the wind

unveiling
the statue comes to life
as day opens

Ric Masten

Contributors

Tapani Ahola
    Järvenpää, Finland http://www.reteaming.com

Joan Barth
    Doylestown, Pennsylvania http://www.jcbcoach.com

David Baum
    Peterborough, New Hampshire http://www.davidbaum.com

Lee Becker
    Lindsborg, Kansas

Ellen Berman
    Merion, Pennsylvania

Michael Bowers
    Alexandria, Virginia

Robert Carroll
    Los Angeles, California

Mary Curran
    deceased

Douglas Doherty
    Nome, Alaska

Timothy Dwyer
    New Orleans, Louisiana

Carol Erickson
> Berkeley, California

John Frykman
> San Francisco, California

Erik Frykman
> Belmont, California

Lars Frykman
> Sonoma, California

Kristin Frykman
> Peterborough, New Hampshire

Ben Furman
> Ymmerstanmaki, Finland http://www.kidskills.com

Diane Gehart
> Fresno, California

William Glasser
> Chatsworth, California

Lisa Hanks-Baxter
> Davis, California

Michael Hoyt
> Mill Valley, California

Jeri Inger
> Portland, Oregon

Zoy Kazan
> Mendocino, California

Jodie Kliman

    Brookline, Massachusetts

Murray Korngold

    San Francisco, California

Jay Lappin

    West Collingswood, New Jersey

Kathleen C. Laundy

    Guilford, Connecticut

Ric Masten

    Palo Colorado Canyon, California http://www.sun-ink.com

Israela Meyerstein

    Baltimore, Maryland

Thorana Nelson

    Mendon, Utah

Fred Piercy

    Blacksburg, Virginia

Phoebe Prosky

    Freeport, Maine

Joellyn Ross

    Cherry Hill, New Jersey and Philadelphia, Pennsylvania

Terry Soo-Hoo

    Hayward, California

Phillip Ziegler

    Oakland, California http://home.igc.org/~ziegler.

About the Editors

John Frykman, Ph.D., is a California-licensed Marriage and Family Therapist, founder of Cypress Institute, an ordained minister, organizer of the first Drug Treatment Program at the Haight Ashbury Free Clinic. He is the author of two books—A New Connection and The Hassle Handbook (Regent Press, Oakland, CA) and many papers and articles. He has three adult children, Kristin, Lars, and Erik, who have all contributed essays to this book and two grandchildren, Charlotte and Kyle.

Thorana S. Nelson, PhD, is an associate professor at Utah State University where she directs the master's program in marriage and family therapy. Although these credentials may make her known professionally, she currently is most pleased to be known as Vic's wife, Travis and Stacy's mom, Taylor and Deryk's gramma. She lives in Utah on the side of a mountain with her husband and two cats.

0-595-29712-9

CPSIA information can be obtained at www.ICGtesting.com
Printed in the USA
BVOW071550221111

276637BV00001B/7/A